Reader Comm

"I want to tell you that the book you gave us is really illuminating and uncovering some very important truths that I have wanted to understand better for a very long time. It is very definitely being used by God to speak to me. Thank you again for passing it on." S. D., OR

"I received the book, 'The Axe Laid to the Root,' as a gift a couple of weeks back and I have been deeply blessed by it. For many years I knew this is the TRUTH but nobody teaches it. The evangelical church has paid so much of attention in the 'old man - new man' theology without realizing that this theology does not work in real life. Then comes along your book ... and suddenly there it is - TRUTH. ... No words can describe the joy in our hearts as we rejoice in finding the 'pearl of great value'. There has been a deep Joy in my soul in reading your book." P. V., Malaysia

"Your book is magnificent!!! It is going to be such a tool for all of us! It is easy to read and gave me such a thrill ..." H.W., KY

"I really enjoyed reading the book, every paragraph that I ingested, my spirit said yes, yes, yes, I could not put it down." M.H., ONT

"It's taken 35 years ... to find your book. It is the best, clearest, purest exposition I have ever read on this topic, and I wish it were possible to inject it directly into the minds and hearts of Christians everywhere." J.M., California

Thank you so much for sending me your book, "The Axe Laid to the Root." On the very first page (Introduction), I heard the best definition of grace I have come across yet: grace is the life of God in us to bring us a life of victory, power and love in Him. I am preparing a lesson on grace to be given at our men's fellowship breakfast. Your book will be a great help in preparing the lesson. R. B., FL

The Axe Laid to the Root

by
Fred Pruitt

authorHOUSE®

AuthorHouse™
1663 Liberty Drive, Suite 200
Bloomington, IN 47403
www.authorhouse.com
Phone: 1-800-839-8640

© 2008 Fred Pruitt. All rights reserved.

No part of this book may be reproduced, stored in a retrieval system, or transmitted by any means without the written permission of the author.

First published by AuthorHouse 9/4/2008

ISBN: 978-1-4259-6694-2 (sc)

Cover illustration by Steve Eilers.

Printed in the United States of America
Bloomington, Indiana

This book is printed on acid-free paper.

Table of Contents

Introduction — vii

Part One: Foundations — 1
- In The Beginning — 3
- Quickened (Enlivened) Out of Death — 4
- What Sin Really Is — 5
- The Most Vital Issue of All – the Self — 8
- The Total Cross — 9
- A Hidden Virus — 12
- We Must Be Born of the Spirit — 15
- The Promise of Life — 17
- God in the Flesh — 19
- Cleansed Consciences — 20
- The Broken Body of Jesus — 21

Part Two: Deliverance from the Law — 27
- The Goal — 29
- The Last Hurdle — 30
- What Is The Self? — 31
- Light At Sinai — 32
- Coming to the Law — 36
- Our Living Experience — 38
- God Is Our Sustenance in the Wilderness — 40
- Law's Dominion – Romans 7:1: — 43
- Coming to the Heart — 44
- Verse 5: — 46
- Verse 6: — 47
- Verse 7: — 47
- Verses 8 – 10: — 48
- Verses 11 & 12: — 49
- Verse 13: — 51

Verse 14:	52
Verses 15 – 20:	54
God Means It for Good	56
Verse 21:	59
Verses 22 – 23:	60
Verse 24:	61
Verse 25:	63
No Condemnation – Romans 8:1	64
Living by the Law is Separation	67
Twoness Supplanted by Oneness	72
What is different?	73
The Law of the Spirit of Life: Romans 8:2	76
What is the law of the Spirit of life?	78
Knowing Is Being	80

Introduction

This short book gets immediately to the heart of the matter, diving right into the depths of our greatest spiritual impediment to a fully functioning life in Christ. We were in a meeting in Atlanta in early 2007, and someone asked the question which surely so many of us think: "Isn't it true that we must all inevitably sin?"

Who of us is able to believe that God through Christ causes us to walk perfectly in His ways, expressing Him only, in the "right now" of our lives? We know we are "supposed to," but most of us think it is an impossible goal and that "grace" is there to sort of cover over the fact that we never measure up.

However, walking in obedience to God is not an impossible goal: in fact, it should be the norm! Though we may think otherwise, grace is not some band-aid that God puts on things to slovenly overlook their occurrence. Grace is the life of God in us to bring us a life of victory, power and love in Him.

Therefore, that is what we will explore in this brief little book. How can we find out who we really are in Christ, and how can we then walk in that knowing? That is what we are after and by God's grace, the reader will discover between the following pages.

*Part One:*
Foundations

In The Beginning

In the beginning, the Genesis story says, God made man (human beings – male and female) in His image. That means that we are made to be that image (God's) reflecting through our human lives. Therefore, to be the image of God means that God has purposed our visibility in order to reveal His invisibility.

Not only from the beginning were we chosen and made to be that image, but as a surety for it, God put Himself into us. The same story that tells us He made us in His image, also tells us that He breathed His own breath into us and we became living beings. So it was the very life or Spirit of God in which we have been one since the absolute beginning.

That means that heaven is in us even deeper than our earthliness. Our bodies were fashioned from the dust of the ground, the story tells us, but the life that came in to animate those bodies was spirit – from heaven. Therefore, that means that man was an original creation in God's universe, a joining of the eternal and the temporal in a oneness.

Then further, in our beginning, the Lord God put us into a safe garden of delights and gave us no law except the commandment not to eat of a certain tree.

Of course, in our innocence, we could not have known what the tree was or what it would do. In addition, the way the tempter represented it made so very much sense to our minds, since wisdom is a thing greatly to be desired and acquired if possible. It seemed so clear that if we got that wisdom for ourselves, we would forever be draped in sumptuous garments. Why, as the serpent said, we would be "as God" Himself!

And we know how the story went from there…

Quickened (Enlivened) Out of Death

With that as background, then, we will skip for now all the ins and outs of the fall, and pick up with Paul speaking to us who are born again in Christ, recounting to us our spiritual history in Ephesians 2:1-3:

> *And you hath He quickened, who were dead in trespasses and sins:*
> *Wherein in time past ye walked according to the course of this world, according to the prince of the power of the air, the spirit that now worketh in the children of disobedience:*
> *Among whom also we all had our conversation in times past in the lusts of our flesh, fulfilling the desires of the flesh and of the mind; and were by nature the children of wrath, even as others.*

Simply put, there are none of us who at one time were not "dead" (to God), and were by <u>nature</u> children of wrath, since we were held in bondage by the one who captured our first parents in the Garden, thus making the whole human race from then on his prisoner from birth.

Of course we are speaking of the great serpent, the dragon of Revelation, the tempter, accuser, and liar from the beginning, known as Satan, Lucifer, Beelzebub, and by many other names. He blinds the minds of those who believe not (2 Cor 3:4), causes us to oppose our own selves (2 Tim 2:25), and it is his very lusts we do when we are his children (John 8:44).

Now of course we also have to know, that this captivity to the god of this world, in which we are held by deception, and from which we cannot escape by our own efforts, manifests itself in evil AND good, because that is the tree from which Adam and Eve ate.

This is an important point, because we are so used to thinking of sin simply as bad or evil things we do. However, those deeds (sins) are the manifestations of sin, which is the indwelling spirit of error who IS sin. Moreover, those deeds can be outwardly "good" or "evil."

The importance of seeing this is that we can begin to take our eyes away from the appearance of good or evil deeds and attitudes, and focus on the spirit from which they originate. This is the beginning of "judging righteous judgment," rather than by the appearance of how something looks on the outside. In other words, we begin seeing things from the inside out, rather than from outside in (John 7:24).

What Sin Really Is

Sin appeared in the universe through Lucifer/Satan, who, as a created angelic being, found himself enamored with himself, and in his self-enamorment, thought himself capable of ascending above his Creator and being "like" God in power and might (Is 14:12-15; Ez 28:13-19). The very name, Lucifer, means "light bearer," and in his proper office he would have been the bearer of God's Light, and the manifestor of blessing and delightful creation in the angelic realm of light and beauty in and for which he was created.

But in his self-deception, Lucifer asserted that God's Light in him was his own self-light (as if the moon could assert that its light was its own, instead of the sun's), and that the power and beauty in which he lived was his own, separate from the Creator Who Himself IS those very realities. Therefore, his light became darkness and the self-giving love of God in which he was created, turned in on itself into self-serving love, which produces pride and eventually wrath (rage), because it can never be fulfilled – it never has enough, is enough, knows enough.

The reason he became pride and wrath is that in his pride of self, self-enamorment, he broke himself off from the Eternal Source of all peace, joy and self-giving Love and Life, in Whom only is fulfillment and rest. His life then forever turned in on himself in eternal unfulfilled desire and need, becoming a raging inferno of eternal hunger and consuming self-desire, a fire that can never be quenched, that seeks only to devour (suck into itself) and to destroy everything in its rage and eternal pain. This is hell and because he lives unto eternity, it is an eternal rage, seeking only to extend and feed itself without end.

We cannot say too much about this because God has not revealed to us much more than this. We cannot say too much about how or why this could be, that is, how or why God, who works all things after the counsel of His own will (Eph 1:11), who cannot lie (Heb 6:18), who cannot tempt (James 1:13), and who is forever fixed as self-giving love, could allow a created angel, with no power or life of his own outside the Life of God, to "rebel" against his own Creator, and seemingly introduce into creation something which God Himself is not.

What Paul tells us is that the Father subjected the creation to vanity for His own purpose, and that through this subjection to vanity – wrongful self-focus, false independent self-relying self producing only futility – we might come to "hope." This is not some vague hope, but rather a twofold specific hope.

The first part is a raising of consciousness, from the disjointed, cracked appearance of this world foisted upon us by the deception of the Tree of Knowledge of Good and Evil, to the truth that everything in creation is perfectly working God's purposes for the benefit of His elect, who love Him and walk in His light.

This is the hope in which we presently walk, esteeming the reproaches of Christ greater riches than any other, because we are seeing Him Who is invisible. And in this hope we realize with joy that here we have no continuing city, because the city we seek and see still afar off, is the city with eternal foundations, whose builder and maker is God. Therefore with eyes opened by the Spirit we see that city, here in our midst (our own middle), and still 'yet to be' in plain sight. This is the hope in which we live, remaining sojourners and wanderers among humanity, even while already dwelling in this moment on the mount to which we have already arrived:

> *But ye <u>ARE COME</u> unto mount Sion, and unto the city of the living God, the heavenly Jerusalem, and to an innumerable company of angels, To the general assembly and church of the firstborn, which are written in heaven, and to God the Judge of all, and to the spirits of just men made perfect, (Heb 11:10, 26-27; 12:22, 23)*

This is the vision that fuels our current hope, which is what Paul calls the "earnest of our inheritance," the Holy Spirit in us as the down payment on what is yet to be. And that 'yet to be' is the second part of that hope in which we walk, because the yet to be will be the unveiling in plain sight and clarity of vision for all, the fullness of the mystery of Christ, fulfilled in every one of us.

The Most Vital Issue of All – the Self

We must come to what it is to be a right kind of self, one not consumed with itself so that it sees only itself in the foreground of everything. This is something simply not possible with men (we are all caught here) – but it IS possible with God! God accomplishes this through the negative of our being caught inescapably in vanity, which builds anguish in us throughout our lives. It is by that very anguish that God causes us first to desire, then to begin to see, and eventually to know the True Joy (God Himself). By and in Him alone, we find our complete release and ultimate liberation. Through that inner full freedom worked in us by the Spirit, God finally delivers the whole universe from corruption by means of the final manifestation of the sons of God. What God reveals in and through His family of sons becomes the liberty of the entire creation (Rom 8:19-22).

And even now we can see that completion in the kingdom of God within us, and we can also see it afar off even within and behind the turmoil and strife of our current world, since John tells us that we are NOW sons of God, though everything concerning our sonship is not yet seen (1 John 3:1-3; Ps 8:4-6).

In addition, we cannot see this after the flesh, i.e., according to natural reason. The scriptures are plain that our state when we are blinded to the Light of God is one of subjection to and of being under the domination of the "god of this world," Satan, whose self-serving falsely independent life we all lived in and expressed (Acts 26:18; 2 Cor 6:14,15; 1 John 3:8,10; 5:19). This comes out of a union between the sin spirit and us, but it is of neither the same quality nor quantity as our union with Christ. Our false imprisonment and slaving bondage by Satan pales in comparison to the glory of the Son in us!

Because even Satan is IN God, so that even in his own rebellious purposes God uses him to accomplish all His will, just as He used Pharaoh to manifest His glory through the plagues in Exodus. Even in our bondage to and captivity by him, he is only in us as a usurper, like a virus, with no true right to us. In the foundation of our being we were created in the image of God (in whom we ALL live and move and have our being – Acts 17:28), and even while held in darkness in our inner selves we are all at our depths the children of God. The light of Christ lights us all (John 1:9), drawing us all to Himself (John 12:39), through which by grace we may respond and come out of darkness into His marvelous light (Col 1:13).

Therefore, this adulterous affair with the sin spirit is a false union, one that really does not fit us, because all of us in our hearts know there is something not right about us. Even though Satan has captured us temporarily, that "Light that lights every man that comes into the world" (John 1:9), continues to make us uncomfortable (as our conscience) in our darkened condition, and we all feel it. Every one of us who are born again in Christ has been in that darkened condition and knows it, but it is that very condition that causes "whosoever will" (Rom 10:13) to call upon the Lord and be saved.

The Total Cross

Now we are getting to our key point. We have stated above the condition of all mankind, which is the condition of us all until we individually experience the new birth, without which no one can or will see the kingdom of God (John 3:3). Now let us briefly look at the Cross, the means of the new birth, so that we may find our solid foundation by which we come to understand how it is we are no longer sinners who must inexorably obey sin, but are now saints, who by grace <u>are now obedient</u> to and expressers of righteousness.

The Cross is prefigured in numerous places in the Old Testament: in Abel's sacrifice, in the flood of Noah, in the sacrifice of Isaac, in the blessing of Esau and Jacob, in the Passover, in the Red Sea, and in many more. One of the most vivid prefigures of the Cross is the story of the serpent in the wilderness, which is mentioned by Jesus in John 3:14.

> *And the LORD sent fiery serpents among the people, and they bit the people; and much people of Israel died.*
> *Therefore the people came to Moses, and said, we have sinned, for we have spoken against the LORD, and against thee; pray unto the LORD, that He take away the serpents from us. And Moses prayed for the people.*
> *And the LORD said unto Moses, Make thee a fiery serpent, and set it upon a pole: and it shall come to pass, that every one that is bitten, when he looketh upon it, shall live.*
> *And Moses made a serpent of brass, and put it upon a pole, and it came to pass, that if a serpent had bitten any man, when he beheld the serpent of brass, he lived. (Numbers 21:6-9)*

It was the serpent who deceived Adam and Eve in Eden, gaining access to them through the fruit of the Tree of Knowledge of Good and Evil. When they ate the fruit, he became the hidden harsh taskmaster in their inner selves, immediately producing in them a self-focusing idolatry, which is spiritual death.

This story of the Israelites in the wilderness is a parable of the same truth. All of humanity has been "bitten" by this serpent, and all became "sick" because of his bite. And the fact that all of mankind has been or is still "sick" from this serpent's bite needs no proof. We only need watch the evening news – or perhaps look even a little closer to home.

But there IS a cure. The cure is, to the natural mind of man, just as absurd in our day of technology, science and innumerable self-focused, self-relying and self-idolizing philosophies and religions, as it must have been to the children of Israel. All they had to do to be cured of the serpent's bite was to behold the brass serpent raised up on a pole in the wilderness.

However, that which the children of Israel were shown and given in a figure or type, we have been given in its fullness and totality in our time in the Cross of Jesus Christ. Jesus of Nazareth, through His death and resurrection, accomplished our total cure, our total deliverance from all the works of the devil. We only need to receive Him by grace through faith as a gift from the Lord to experience this cure for ourselves.

Now, before we move into an explanation of what this "cure" is in its totality, let me one more time unequivocally state what the source of this sickness is, and what is its chief symptom.

A Hidden Virus

There has been a hidden virus in every one of us from birth, which infects us all from our inner core in our unbelief, so that we not only commit the acts, thoughts or intents of sins, we ARE sin! It does not matter if we are the most moral of men, or the most base and crude, because when we are living our lives from the hidden inner basis of darkness – self-for-self – it is out of a condition of sin coming from the "god" of sin.

That condition runs the gamut. We are each of us, in any walk of life or economic station, the same in the eyes of God, when through unbelief pride of self is at the inner core. We have inherited this condition of sin from our first parents. Through the succeeding millennia, this false tree has reached a great level of sophistication. It has built a mighty building throughout the whole world to which all the world gives homage. This false building of sin, this false tree, is what we call <u>independent, self-relying, self-motivating, self-loving self</u> – a false consciousness of self that, like its father Lucifer in Isaiah 14, would be "like the Most High"; it would ascend above God Himself, and would BE God!

Let us talk straight talk here. I am not speaking of a point of theology here. This is the absolute root of the tree. This is what Jesus chops out with His axe! He has laid His axe to the root of the false tree, containing Satan and all his lies! He chops it out of US!

That serpent's seed, sown in Adam and Eve and then passed to all their progeny, has grown into a great tree that permeates every inch of our world. It is the seed of "I, Me, Mine," a false building of self that imagines (wrongly) that it is its own center of being.

Everything in the world is subservient to it. It is the deepest and most pervasive perversion and abomination there can be in the universe, because it is the devil's own, and yet it is even more an abomination in that it can so easily portray itself as holy and righteous and appear full of light and peace, and often presents itself so.

This is "Mystery Babylon," the "Tower of Babel," the "leaven" that leavens the whole lump, Achan's "accursed thing," and many other scriptural descriptions. It is the monster of the devil, the building and body of sin. It is the Antichrist, and people are greatly misguided to spend all their time looking for clues for who is the Antichrist who is coming, when he has always been living in everyone who does not abide in the Son. He is they. And he has always been around.

Humanity did not originate this lie, nor is it capable on its own of recognizing it. We have been hoodwinked to think we are each just our little islands of self, alone in the universe, when the reality is completely the opposite. We are each branches on one human vine, all joined together and to the source of the vine. However, Lucifer deceived himself into an imaginary independence, and infected us with the same deception. He usurped the fire of self in him so that he was to himself as if he was his own self-creating fire, his own self-sustaining life – that he was his own light, his own wisdom, his own power, and his own goodness. Therefore, he need "serve" no other God beyond himself, since he asserted his own self-sufficiency, his own self-deification.

By that eternal irrefutable rebellion he cast off the only Source of Life there is, and forever became self-loving self-serving love, love turned inward instead of outward, which is unrelenting anguish. And it is Satan's hell-life that we formerly manifested by our inner participation, and that same hell-life in which we stood in mortal danger of falling into forever, except for the Cross. It is this same hell-life that the whole world stands in danger of eternally, if it turns not from it.

It was this great need on the part of creation that had been involuntarily subjected to vanity, a need so great that it required death in the heart of the Godhead itself to fulfill it (and if it required DEATH in the Deity, then eternal death must have been at stake). It was so wrenching and desperate a need that it drew the Lamb of God from heaven to earth, from God-ness to Man-ness, from the eternal into the temporal.

The need had nothing to do with saving the temporal life, but with the eternal, because the fall was not from eternal into temporal. The fall into the temporal, so that we are transfixed by it and cannot turn away from it, is true enough, but it is not the source of our fall.

Nor was it simply a fall into ignorance or forgetfulness. Though instigated through the outer world, the world it affected was the inner world, the center from which everything springs. As the scripture says, *"Keep thy heart with all diligence, for out of it are the springs of life,"* (Prov 4:23), and that was where the fall occurred. Our hearts, innermost selves, darkened. We fell from light into darkness, from truth into error, from righteousness into sin, from God into Satan. We fell into an error that springs from an eternal, though false, spirit source.

In addition, the hypnosis of this lie is simply something we cannot escape on our own. We cannot patch this up. We cannot turn over a new leaf. There are no new attitudes we can pretend we have to make us more like God. We cannot find and live by the right philosophy. We cannot work up the right motivations.

Something completely new has to occur. That was what Jesus said to Nicodemus and many others. It is futile to put new wine into old wineskins. It is a different type of life from anything we have ever known before. This is Life originating not in ourselves, but from beyond us, and yet found in us! It is this new life which Jesus said He Himself was, that which "cometh down from heaven," (John 6:33,50), that we receive in the new birth, and without which one cannot know heaven, because that IS the heavenly life, God Himself, coming to dwell in man.

We Must Be Born of the Spirit

Now we are ready to understand what the new birth is.

When we receive Christ by the Spirit, we are first mainly conscious of His forgiveness of our sins, our outer deeds, by the effects and working of His blood. This is a great mystery, because we cannot possibly understand how blood, even the blood of Christ, is able to do this. But God gets our attention by means of our selfish acts and thoughts, and in some way brings us to a desire for repentance. In that repentance, which means a "turning away," or a "change of mind," the Spirit of God meets us with wondrous and miraculous grace. Somehow we know that something amazing and completely different (out of this world!) has happened to us, something we could not possibly have anticipated.

Even though we are not yet aware of what has happened to us, for the first time we begin to know a deeper sense of peace as we are overtaken by a new affection. A new love we have never known before begins to flow out of us, first toward God and then toward others. Scales drop from our eyes, and for the first time we begin to see the kingdom of God. Moreover, inwardly, in our minds and hearts, we begin to experience what really is a miracle – the forgiveness of sins.

Now let us understand what this forgiveness of sins is, because it is not something to pass over lightly.

First, God did not change or go anywhere. He remained, and remains, eternally the same in Love. It is man that went away. God is the Father of the Prodigal Son. He longs continually after him whole time of his wandering. It is the son who has left to spend his inheritance in riotous living, while the father, whose heart is always with his son in concern and hope, waits at home until the son comes to his senses in the middle of a pen full of pig dung.

In the Garden, it was Adam and Eve who suddenly felt fear and shame, not the Lord God. The wrath came alive in them! God Himself is only Love, Whose arm is always outstretched toward us all, Who would have none of us perish, Who sent His son to seek and gather all who are lost into Himself.

When Adam and Eve sinned and as a result hid among the trees in the Garden, God expressed no anger toward them. Instead, He seeks them, calling them by name: *"Adam, where are you?"* Of course, God knew where they were and what they had done. Even when they come forward and acknowledge that they had broken His one prohibition, still He expresses neither anger nor wrath toward them, but only compassion and provision as He tells them the consequences of their choice. He even clothes them before He sends them out of the Garden on their (our) long road back to Him.

And it was not because of disobedience to an arbitrary commandment, as if God just picked something they could not do, and because they didn't do what He said, the punishment was death. Obedience is the point, but not because obedience is the point, but because obedience points to Life. Likewise, disobedience did not lead to death just because it was disobedience, but because the thing they chose to do was Death itself. Eating the fruit of the false Tree awakened the wrath, because the Tree hiddenly contained the god of wrath, who they received within themselves when they took their bites.

The Promise of Life

But even though they have knowingly disobeyed His only prohibition, the Lord God doesn't come all in a huff, storming around in the garden looking for them, ready to rain down fire and destruction on their heads. Rather than rage or disgust, instead there is a resolved sadness on the part of the Lord God. He knows that something has been opened that must now be allowed to run its course. But He also knows the outcome, because on the spot He speaks the first Promise of the Redeemer into their very hearts, reintroducing Himself into that holy sanctuary that had been invaded and violated: *"And I will put enmity between thee and the woman, and between thy seed and her seed; it shall bruise thy head, and thou shalt bruise His heel."* (Gen 3:15)

That promise is the first foreshadowing of the Redeemer to come, the Bruiser of the Serpent, who was a Lamb slain before there was a sinner to redeem, and has been from the foundation of the world (Rev 13:8). Not only has He been the Lamb slain in eternity, but He has been that same Lamb in all humanity from that time-moment in Adam and Eve where they met the Lord God in the cool of the day, the Lord calling them out of their hiding place. The Lord God spoke His Word not only toward the future, pertaining to their descendents and Jesus Christ who was to come, but He spoke it as an immediate response to what the serpent had done. The serpent had tricked them into allowing his entrance into their humanity through their disobedience, but so too had the Redeemer re-entered humanity to fight for it from the moment the serpent slithered in and set up camp. God has never abandoned us, and through Christ has always been every person's inner word of hope, so that from the beginning until now in whatever time or place, He has been available and certain to anyone who would call out to Him (Acts 10:34,35).

God does not change; He is only Love. However, we changed, and wrath became our condition. And this has effects. Under the power of this god of wrath, we find ourselves opposing ourselves. We are ashamed of ourselves. We are guilty and we know it even if we will not accept it. And the more we lie, cheat and steal, whether literally or figuratively, the more we are guilty and out of sorts, though we try to cover it up with all sorts of methods – alcohol, drugs, education, houses, religion, philosophy, hobbies, sex – anything we can do to take our attention off our inner misery of heart and mind. Throughout life it accumulates, building a great structure in us that we either try to keep hidden from everybody else by pretending we are moral, loving people, (because we all know that is what we SHOULD be), or else we cast off all pretense and live evil to the uttermost. And all this produces fear, torment, and wrath in us, just as it came alive in Adam and Eve the moment they swallowed the fruit.

God in the Flesh

But then in the fullness of time, the Bruiser of the Serpent appeared in the flesh, as *"Jesus came into Galilee, preaching the gospel of the kingdom of God, and saying, The time is fulfilled, and the kingdom of God is at hand: repent ye, and believe the good news."* (Mark 1:14, 15)

When Jesus came into Galilee, everywhere He walked He encountered those who were hurting and almost crushed to powder under the great weight of the accumulation of sins and guilt in their lives. Because He was the love of God in human flesh, their great need draw out His Father's compassion. To the man sick of the palsy He said, *"Son, be of good cheer, thy sins are forgiven thee"* (Mat 9:2). To a prostitute who washed His feet with her hair and tears, He said again, *"Thy sins are forgiven"* (Luke 7:48).

Jesus demonstrated that God's heart is grace and reconciliation, not the wrath and anger we have all feared. For this is God's real heart toward all His lost sheep: *"Come now, and let us reason together, saith the LORD: though your sins be as scarlet, they shall be as white as snow; though they be red like crimson, they shall be as wool"* (Isa 1:18).

The commission Jesus declared fulfilled in the synagogue in Nazareth brought out this very heart and purpose of God, which was not retribution and punishment, but forgiveness and freedom: *"The Spirit of the Lord GOD is upon Me; because the LORD hath anointed Me to preach good tidings unto the meek; He hath sent Me to bind up the brokenhearted, to proclaim liberty to the captives, and the opening of the prison to them that are bound; To proclaim the acceptable year of the LORD ..."* (Isa 61:1,2)

And this is the love of God toward us, in that, while we were dead in trespasses and sins, while we were enemies in our hearts and living in pride and wrath, while we were the ungodly and did all we could to rebel and wreak havoc in our own lives and the lives of those around us, He nevertheless reached out to us to "first love us," to "choose us" before we chose Him. He sent Another to take our place and redeem us by the mystery of His broken Body and shed Blood. This is the unfathomably loving heart of God toward us.

Cleansed Consciences

I have taken a long time to make this point because so many of us are not able to shake the idea that God is always displeased and angry with us. The life of Jesus life portrayed in the gospels dispels that notion, but the reason we have such difficulty believing and apprehending it so that it is our own, is because of this lifelong accumulation of guilt and self-loathing (even if covered up by self-pride). We can only see God through this veil of guilt and shame, which is where the blood of forgiveness comes in. His blood is the total cleansing of our consciences before God, by which we experience the peace of God. We begin to know this peace within ourselves through the blood, which mysteriously wipes away the residual effects of every sinful act or purpose we have ever done or considered. God remembers them no more forever.

Our conscience is forever wiped clean and made new in innocence, in the blood of the Eternal Lamb. Not only do we know God's forgiveness in the blood of Jesus, but because the blood is a purging of our consciences, a doing away forever of a consciousness of and toward sin, we return to childlike innocence in our hearts and minds! The tabernacle sacrifices could not accomplish this permanent doing away with a consciousness of sin. Nevertheless, they were always pointing beyond themselves to the blood of Jesus, whose once for all sacrifice, eternal in the heavens, purges our consciences forever from the effects of sin. By that purging, we are now able to come before the throne of grace with a holy _boldness_, which we could not do while the consciousness of our sins and iniquities kept us as the children of Israel who could not touch the mountain, lest they die.

No one can come into His true presence in a consciousness of sin. However, now it is a fact that we may be bold with God, since our sins, which were an impassible gulf between us, have been totally removed. Because of the blood of Christ, the Father has brought us into the full fellowship of being sons, with all the rights, privileges and responsibilities of being those sons.

The Broken Body of Jesus

Now we come to the Body of Jesus Christ, the Bread of Heaven, by the breaking of which the totality of our salvation is fully secured. As I stated above, the spirit of unrighteousness invaded in our inner center through Adam, and has been our hidden motivator in all that we have done in our unbelief. (Even then, we are not outside the plan of the Father. Even while under the captivity of

Satan, God has known us from before the foundation of the earth, and has "separated us from our mother's womb," with the intent, as with Paul, to one day, "reveal His Son" <u>in us</u>! [Gal 1:15, 16])

This is where we see how appropriate the story of the brazen serpent is, because what Moses hints at in types and shadows God brings to pass in totality and plain sight through the breaking of the precious body of Jesus.

As I have been saying, sins, or outer deeds, thoughts and attitudes, are not our real problem. The blood has taken care of that problem. Since our deeds and thoughts are the first things most of us are aware of, we think that those things are God's main issue with us. He wants us, we think, to be "good," (to use children's language), and we try but sometimes we are bad anyway. Most people think that is the sum total of our problem. If we can now do good things, good works, we think, God will be pleased with us.

Now of course God does seek in us the fruit of righteousness, but we do not find the origin of that fruit by improving or guarding our deeds and thoughts. We find it in our spirit center. Through our unbelief, we have been invaded and run from within by a false god, who has held us in captivity to sin. Nothing we are able to do can fix that. We must instead have a total inner change, from the false god to the True God. That is our only hope of Life.

When a person dies, his spirit leaves that body and it becomes no more than a decaying shell. I remember one of the first funerals I attended after I knew the Lord, how it was so obvious to me that the true life of my brother was not his body. Looking at his body lying there in the casket, I saw it had been nothing more than a shell. I knew my brother was no longer there, and now the true man, his spirit, had gone on to be with the Lord.

When Jesus hung from the Cross, according to the Father's plan and with Jesus' foreknowledge, (which is why the struggle in Gethsemane was so difficult), it was more than just a representative sacrifice, as the animal temple sacrifices had been through the Law of Moses. The blood of bulls and goats merely pointed at what was to come, but in themselves could accomplish nothing. Certainly God honored those who participated in those sacrifices with faith, but in Jesus the veil of the temple is split in two and we are able to see now without the veil plainly and clearly what God has done – and Who and where He is!

Our problem was that we had been invaded, captured and enslaved, so that one who essentially had no right to us, had stolen us and bound us in evil, from whom we had no power to escape. Someone stronger than he and we had to come to accomplish a rescue, to separate us from the spirit of rebellion that blinded our minds and hearts. And because his spirit inhabited our spirits in our bodies, something which we cannot see according to the flesh but can only know by the Spirit, the only means of escape is by death, because a spirit only departs the body when the body dies.

When Jesus cried on the Cross, *"My God, my God, why hast thou forsaken Me"*, He was entering His uttermost intercession for us. As I said above, we were not sinners simply because we did bad things, but we did bad things because we were sinners, because in our inner center, having been infected by Satan's own sin nature within us, we WERE SIN! In order for the Father to fully secure our salvation, it was not enough to just remove the individual transgressions (sins) and their effects, but more importantly He had to destroy SIN at its innermost root in us. And the root of it is the spirit of sin in each of us, who has deceived us with this great lie about who we are – that we are independent, self-relying, self-originating selves who determine our own lives, when all along we were Satan's unwitting dupes, deceived and deceiving others.

Therefore the Father put upon Jesus the Son all that we had become, cast Him down into death into the deepest depths, as far down as sin would take us, into the bottomless pit of chaos, despair and sorrow, which we call hell. Jesus, who had known every single temptation every human being has ever experienced, yet without having entered into sin, gave up His own righteousness from God, and then the Father caused Him to be <u>all that we were</u>! Just as it was gazing at a serpent lifted up on a pole in the wilderness that caused the Israelites to be healed from the bite of the serpent, even so Jesus became the serpent lifted up on the pole for all time and eternity to see. HE BECAME SIN FOR US! *"For He [God the Father] hath made Him [Jesus] to be sin for us, who knew no sin; that we might be made the righteousness of God in Him."* (2 Cor 5:21)

What we were – SIN – He became, that in His resurrection by the Holy Spirit, the same Spirit that raised Jesus from the dead, now raises us from the dead, and we become, by His work – not by anything we do – the righteousness of God. Because when Jesus' body died and His spirit left His body, even though the Father let the spirit of sin work its full work in Him to the point of Sin taking Him into the heart of the flaming eternal wrath, IT COULD NOT HOLD HIM.

By a power not His own, since He had completely laid down His life unto death, trusting the Father would not allow Him to see corruption, Jesus was bodily raised forever to the right hand of God. By His accomplishment He was then given a name above every name, and forever became the Captain of our salvation Who is always leading captivity captive and multitudes of sons to the glory of God. He joined us in our fallen humanity and redeemed it, not only for our benefit in this world, but even more, for *"an eternal weight of glory"* (2 Cor 4:17), in which we are even this moment embraced in the bosom of the Father in Christ, and sitting with Him on the right hand of God. That is the life that works in us now, so that we who were formerly slaves of sin, are now bond slaves of righteousness and live in His favor. Our members, our humanity, which were formerly given to unrighteousness and selfishness, now belong to Christ and are the members of Christ. He has made us to become the very living expression of righteousness in the present moment.

Therefore, it is bordering on blasphemy to continue calling ourselves sinners, after so great a work by so great a sacrifice has been accomplished. How DARE WE call ourselves sinners, for if we are, then is Christ's death of any effect? The resurrection of Jesus is also OUR resurrection unto righteousness, and by His life we have been called (and when we are called by God it means we ARE) SAINTS!

This is no mere new wine in old wineskins. This is a completely new creation, not a patched up repair job, but new wine in new wineskins, in which ALL THINGS have become new, and all old things have passed away, and we come near to doing despite unto the Spirit of grace (Heb 10:29), to call what God has cleansed common (Acts 10:15).

> *Purge out therefore the old leaven, that ye may be a new lump, as ye are unleavened. For even Christ our Passover is sacrificed for us: Therefore let us keep the feast, not with old leaven, neither with the leaven of malice and wickedness; but with the unleavened bread of sincerity and truth. (1 Cor 5:7,8)*

Part Two:
Deliverance from the Law

The Goal

We are gearing up now to make the final push into the liberty of love, through the wilderness of self-reliance and its impenetrable brick walls by the law, to our ultimate goal. Even though while in the body we have yet to come over the horizon into full sight, the liberty of Christ is still more marvelous and full of grace in the present moment than we can ever comprehend.

We come to an inner complete loss of all things including our very selves, and in that nothingness we discover we only truly know one thing: God through Christ in us. We disappear into Him and we find Him the Only One, the All in all, and in His glory what would we claim for our separate selves? There is only His light, shining on and revealing everything, and there is nothing else. How could we begin to stand?

But then by unbelievable yet unfailing grace, we surprisingly and joyfully find ourselves again. We find that right in the middle of our own person, in the "I" that we each are, Christ has penetrated even there! Therefore, now in this seeing of God only, suddenly our true self arrives. In a paradox, we see only God and suddenly we appear. By the Cross and a new life (Christ, self-giving love) in us, replacing the old (Satan, self-absorbed love), what rises in resurrection is a new self no longer consumed with itself, which now shines as a clear light without restraint into the world.

That is the "Land of Promise" as it pertains to this life. We are the grace of God in Jesus Christ shining into the world in whatever capacity God wills by us. We come into possessing our possessions when we in some sense come into a personal consciousness of grace and power by a union of selves in our daily living, in which God not only wills by us and as us, but also works by and as us, and we know His working.

The Last Hurdle

Now we come to the last major hurdle in reaching that Land. We call it independent self, some writers just self, others the flesh, self-reliance, self-effort, and the list goes on.

If we are at this threshold, then we know we have no strength left. More "trying" is no longer an option. We have finally become aware that there really are giants and great walled cities in the land and we truly are as grasshoppers in our own sight. We have finally realized we cannot take the land by anything we have or are. And this revelation, that we can do nothing whatsoever of ourselves, which at the time seems so awful and negative, is the absolute bottom, the total death, from which new life rises.

It is sadly true that many have settled with, "We must always try our best to live as God wants us to, but we always have to remember we sin every day," or some similar notion, which is a sad turning away with the ten spies to walk more years in the wilderness (Numbers chapters 13 & 14). However, Paul's Romans 7 is plaintively asking: Is it possible to cut to the chase with humanity's deepest problem, our so-called "fatal flaw,", or "sin" according to the gospel, and cut it out at the root, so that we now habitually live without sin unto God and bear fruit by Him?

Or are we not we reaching here a bit beyond our capacity and being very presumptuous? We all know that "nobody's perfect except Jesus." Still that is the question

Paul is faced with in his, "I want to but I can't," dilemma of the famous Romans chapter 7. This is not academic. Paul described this so that we might know it when we arrive at the same juncture, because this is something everyone of us faces.

What Is The Self?

Before we move into taking this bull by the horns, we have to cover briefly one more basic issue. It is the issue of the self itself, the absolute core of the matter. What are we? What is the self?

No one could possibly define every aspect, but one certain basic aspect is that the self is fire. How can we say that? We start with the word from Deuteronomy, which says, *"Our God is a consuming fire."* (Deut 4:24).

Our selves can only exist as selves in Him in God's own Self-existence (being), since His existence is all there is. Therefore, that is the sense in which I take liberty to say, if God, Who is the True I AM, is fire, then so are we. We are fire of His Fire. He is the only Life, the only True Person there is, and so we can only be existing as created and sustained in His very being. *The spirit of man is the candle of the LORD, searching all the inward parts of the belly.* (Prov 20:27)

Then what do we mean by fire?

It is the fire of self. In human beings, in the physical we know it as heat, sexual desire, or hunger. In the emotions and reason fire manifests as passion or inspiration. In the spirit, it is life reaching out of itself to find a reflection of or extension of itself. Self is a fire that has to have fuel for its burning. It is a born need, a desire that we must fulfill.

However, fire burns things up. It destroys. Fire consumes everything placed into it or within its reach. It has no mercy, because a fire that burns hot enough consumes everything around. So if God is consuming fire, fire that burns everything up and destroys it in that consumption, then how can God be love, which we might say is the result of fire, but not fire itself: as fire gives light, heat, provision?

What is it that transforms us inside ourselves? Can that fire that has burned within me, which has been consuming everybody and everything around me, by everything being ultimately for me – MY family, MY job, MY career, MY faith, MY spirituality, MY walk, MY spouse, MY hopes, MY fears, MY talents, MY flaws, MY God – actually be changed and redirected so that that fire's same wants and needs are now wed into the love of God in which the fire becomes satisfied and thus overflowing with life for others, instead of other's lives for me? Is it possible?

Light At Sinai

The burning bush at Mt. Sinai is a perfect picture of our answer (Exodus chapter 3). A bush is aflame, but it is not being consumed. The voice coming out of the bush identifies Himself to Moses as, "I AM THAT I AM." It is a picture of life in harmony with God, with man being in an inwardly conscious union of God and man, signified by the flame burning in a regular normal bush. The fire that does not consume the bush is – I AM – God, and the bush that is not consumed and yet is burning in the fire of God and out of which the Voice of God speaks, is us. He lives in us as us. (*"When you see me, you see the Father,"* said Jesus. John 14:9)

Some time later, when Moses brings the people out of Egypt back to the same mountain, the whole mountain seemed to be a flame of fire to the Israelites and they were terribly frightened. Moses had given them strict instructions not to touch it under penalty of death. However, Moses had no restrictions on him. He could go up into the darkness, flames and smoke, where God was, and come down without penalty (Exodus chapters 19 and 20). How could that be?

Moses' previous encounter at Mt. Sinai had changed his inner consciousness from separation into a personal realization of union with God, so that he began to know that his speaking was God speaking. He has lost his consciousness of independence, self-reliance, flesh-mindedness and self-absorption through the desert, and at the burning bush he saw a picture of himself as God was revealing Himself in him, "I AM." His fire of self that years before had sought to be somebody, to do something, to become something, to show everybody who he was, had burned hot enough to murder an Egyptian overseer, and Moses ended up fleeing the king he sought to overthrow.

But at Sinai that Moses is gone, having perished in the desert, and this is a new Moses that has discovered by the flame in the bush, "Not I, but Christ." The bush that burns with God's fire but without being consumed, demonstrates how the fire of God is in us not to enslave us or put us into bondage, but through the Spirit to release us into outgoing light and blessing through the glory and the freedom of liberated right self in us. This liberated, "right self," is Christ in us as one person with us, so that we living are He living, and yet it is we!

Someone asked us recently at a church in Florida, "If God comes into us to be our very life, do we stop being ourselves? What happens to us?" The reply was, Christ comes into us and lives our lives in order that we might become ourselves. He makes me to become the real "me."

That sounds confusing, but is that not the picture on the mount? A common bush burns with a fire that is so bright it attracts Moses' attention far below. It is a regular normal mountainside bush, but it glows with a glory not its own, is blazing yet not burning up, and the Word of God speaks out of the midst of it. That is an exact picture of our life in Christ.

The fire is the fire of self, both God's and ours, intertwined as one person living, always living in the continuously burning fire. There is in the fire of self a desire always to go out of itself to seek what it will be and to be it. It is dangerous material, this self, because of the fact that it is fire and ultimately power, and hypnotizing to boot.

God has eternally determined in Himself to be love for others, so that the blaze of Self is always coming from the Lamb slain in the midst of the Throne. Therefore, since at the center and heart of God there is eternally a Cross, He has thus made Himself eternally safe in love, so that He wills only love, He purposes only love, and His acts are only love.

But what about the human self, which is also compounded of this same fire? Something has to make my fire safe. I have to be made safe to take up the fullness of myself, with all its powers and potentials. Satan had formerly taken that self-fire and turned it in on itself in us, so that inwardly we burned with pride of self and self-adoration, and were hiddenly for ourselves, even in seeking God, because we were wanting God to make US something! It is the hiss of the snake, but seems so innocent from our own viewpoint.

That is why the Israelites could not ascend or even touch the mountain, or they would die. The mountain engulfed by the flame of fire on top and surrounded by the thick darkness, was both the dwelling place of God and of being an affirmed right self in Him, as Moses had found. The Israelites had not yet learned what God had shown Moses – that only His life in them could make them safe and free to find themselves in freedom, truth and love, and to be inwardly transformed into those who give themselves to others instead of taking from them. In their consciousness, they were still flesh or self-minded, still being the center of their own lives, and the wilderness and the law hadn't yet made them ready to be themselves in full bloom.

They could not even touch the mountain or it would kill them, because "no flesh shall enter my presence." Now, that obviously is not talking about human physical flesh, because Moses went up in his body. In different ways, so did Enoch and Elijah. So it is the consciousness of flesh, of independence, of self-idolizing, of self-focus, of gaining and getting for myself (no matter how subtle), that cannot approach God.

Let us get this straight. The flesh the Bible speaks of when it is referring to our waywardness and rebellion, is not the physical body, nor is it the human soul, with its emotions and human reasoning faculties. It is our fallen consciousness of independence, and all its ramifications, which we identify as "the flesh." (Keeping that in mind will make everything we go over below much clearer.)

This is the consciousness of sin – "I'm myself alone and am in charge of myself" – with which our whole race has been infected since Adam. This is a devil originated and upheld falsehood, hiding the inner fact that he is the one running our show, and the whole world system is based on this lie. And we all live in it even as believers until we are delivered in our minds by the Spirit by an inner awareness of who He is in us, and we in Him – "He that is joined to the Lord is one spirit," (1 Cor 6:17) – and we are now able to, *"be no more children … but may grow up into Him in all things, even Christ."* (Eph 4:14, 15)

Coming to the Law

In part one, we went over the work of the Cross through Jesus' blood and body. First, we saw how we found forgiveness of sins and a purging of our consciences in His blood. Then we discovered how Jesus' broken body delivered us from the bondage of the devil. This devil had invaded our minds and hearts by trickery, convincing us we were just ourselves functioning alone, our own originators of good or evil, holiness or sin. However, all the while in this spirit we did his works of darkness, of self for self, whether in supposed good or actual evil. And then we showed that in the death and resurrection of Jesus Christ we were delivered from that spirit of sin, removed from his domain, taken from hell to heaven, from darkness to light, and by that resurrection we are no longer slaves or expressers of sin, since he who IS Sin, has no place in us anymore. Therefore we cannot rightly continue being called "sinners," because we are now partakers of the divine nature (2 Pet 1:4), which is Christ expressing His righteousness by means of our human selves. This means that in Jesus Christ through His Cross, we are now made saints of God (2 Cor 5:21). This is the true canonization, and is a common sainthood to all in Christ.

However, there is another aspect that we did not cover and from which we were delivered in the Cross, and that is our deliverance from the Law. That is the least understood of our deliverances, and the final key to our total liberation.

We see that the path the Israelites had to take to the Promised Land, after the escape by the plagues in Egypt and the Red Sea, before they can go up to possess the Land, is through the wilderness and a confrontation with the Law.

Their exodus from Egypt and rescue in the Red Sea is their baptism into Moses, who was Christ to them in the form of the Law. They have escaped the harsh taskmaster of Egypt, the devil/pharaoh who held them in captivity. The Lamb's blood of the Passover has cleansed them, and they have been baptized into Him in the cloud and the sea, the Spirit and the water (1 Cor 10:1-4). Figuratively, they are as new born Christian babes, who have been given a vision of the new life that awaits them, and lost in the joy of such unbelievable and surprising grace, set out with grit and determination to attain the goal of the fullness of God's kingdom.

Only soon they find themselves in a wilderness, and someone is thundering down at them, telling them they must live up to the standards that are now being shown to them – things not mentioned back in Egypt!

Our Living Experience

This Bible story of the Israelites in the wilderness is a picture of how it is with us in our life in Christ. In my case, when I found Jesus I went absolutely nuts! Being born again changed everything, and I began to see things from that new perspective. I was enthralled in a newly found joy of life, as if I was seeing everything in the world for the very first time. It is said that to be born of God's Spirit is like becoming an innocent little child all over again, and I found out first hand that is true.

Janis and I had bought a Volkswagen bus a few months before our conversion. It was a 1959, with the old 40hp engine. A previous owner had modified the bus into a makeshift camper by cutting out the middle third of the roof, replacing the space with a plywood doghouse-looking structure. Inside we could stand up in the rear and feel roomy. Outside however, the thick, heavy plywood added a huge amount of weight for the already strained little engine to push. To make matters worse, it created a flat surface for near perfect wind resistance, adding even more to the strain on the engine. This made highway driving relaxing, but oh so slow. We could not go faster than 50 mph unless we were going downhill with a tailwind. When we drove it to California, the police stopped us twice on the interstate for going too SLOW!

However, back to this story. As I said, I went crazy for Jesus. I went to the Christian bookstore and bought every bumper sticker they had and plastered them all over the bus. I bought little New Testaments to pass out. However, what took the cake home was this. Janis came out of the house one day and found me on top of the bus with a bucket of fire engine red paint and a large brush. "What are you doing up there?" she demanded.

"I'm painting a big red JESUS on the bus!" I replied proudly. And I did, JESUS in twelve inch high RED letters, front and back, so that coming or going, people KNEW we loved Jesus! (Hitchhikers' thumbs would go down faster than lightning when they saw us approach.)

She was not as proud of it as I was, I don't think. Poor wives, what they sometimes have to put up with!

But my point is how crazily enthusiastic I became when I was born again. Nothing seemed impossible. Miracles happened. Prayers were answered. Everything was new and electric! The air was different!

After a few months of that and our subsequent move to California, one day a brother said to me, "Fred, with that big Jesus sign on your bus, you've put yourself in front of others as an example. Now you're going to have to get your life in order so you can live up to it!"

And, like the children of Israel who replied to Moses when he came back from the mountain with the law said, *"All that the LORD hath said will we do, and be obedient"* (Ex 24:7), I said the same. I fulfilled it as well as they did. (Not very well!)

All I could hear after that for a long time was how I needed to be closer to God by becoming somehow "better," and becoming better became my elusive sole interest. I seemed to hear it from all my brothers and sisters, as well as our preachers, teachers and counselors. Becoming this elusive "better person" logically seemed to be a sure fire way to the prize of closeness with God. How nice to have a path! Just do these things, and you are there. Oh yes, I hear you and I am on the bandwagon. I am going to pray. I am going to storm heaven until I get an answer. I am going to study. I am going to love my family more, and be more giving. I am going to become a thoughtful, listening, loving person. Just apply this, apply that. Keep these principles.

And I tried and I tried, and the more I tried, the harder it became, and the more condemned I felt. After a time that first "joy of my salvation" went away. My tears were no longer tears of joy, but instead became tears of, "Where is my God?"

God Is Our Sustenance in the Wilderness

At this point, we are tempted to think we must have taken a wrong turn somewhere, that THIS could not be God's plan. On the contrary, I found God leads us this way and engineers our bout with the Law. During this time, the Spirit leads us in a fiery pillar in the night and a cloudy pillar by day. Visions and clarity come in the night, when it is dark and we are alone. In the day there are all sorts of other voices and sights that cloud our vision, but we are still just as led by the Spirit every step! The clarity of the night is obscured in the light, and here we learn that we are led and sustained not of ourselves, beyond our own mind or understanding. We walk on day by day, not knowing the end of the journey or even the next step, but our shoes do not wear out, and every day there is always enough to eat and water to drink. It seems like we are in the wilderness of our own making, (oh, if I was just more dedicated, if I was more loving, if I was this or that!), but we actually <u>are</u> in the wilderness where God has led us and continually sustains us. We are being taught by living experience He is our real bread and He is our real water. We are learning to eat and drink only Christ!

The best way to get that across is by privation, as the Spirit drove Jesus into the wilderness to be tempted of the devil, whereby the Father proved Himself in Jesus. It is about finding God the upholder of all, as All in all <u>in us</u>. It is about God proving Himself to us and in us, that He is the Faithful One, He Who causes all things to be, and is our upholder in all things – from the ins and outs of our moment by moment breathing, to the stars coursing through their paths in the heavens. We see the same process of failure and privation to glory in many of the stories: Abraham, Isaac, Jacob, Joseph, Moses, David most particularly, where all of them found the sufficiency of God in the deserts where God led them.

And even while we remain in the wilderness, despite the fact that we might still be living in flesh or self-mindedness in our immaturity and ignorance, God sees us the whole time of our wilderness days by that oddly expressed word of Balaam the prophet. Balaam is essentially out only for personal gain and the King of Moab hires him to curse the whole of Israel camped in the valley. Balaam is instead taken by the Spirit of God, surprising and enraging the King of Moab when he pronounces only blessing on Israel in one of the most glorious passages in scripture.

Balaam the prophet speaks:

> *God is not a man, that He should lie; neither the son of man, that He should repent: hath He said, and shall He not do it? or hath He spoken, and shall He not make it good?*
> *Behold, I have received commandment to bless: and He hath blessed; and I cannot reverse it.*
> *He hath not beheld iniquity in Jacob, neither hath He seen perverseness in Israel: the LORD his God*

is with him, and the shout of a king is among them.
God brought them out of Egypt; He hath as it were the strength of an unicorn.
Surely there is no enchantment against Jacob, neither is there any divination against Israel: according to this time it shall be said of Jacob and of Israel, What hath God wrought! (Num 23:19-23)

Well were the heathen warned, "This is the work of the Living God!" Those who look on Christ's Church and the people of God only outwardly, and see only the disagreement, quarreling, failures, hypocrisy and other universal human frailties, miss a miracle happening in their midst.

The Living God sees His people through His own righteousness, which is Jesus Christ, who has taken all who abide in Him into His bosom. The Father loves the Son and we appear in the Son and are thus loved of the Father. He does not see a spot of evil in those who are His own. Because His eyes, the eyes of the One who lives in us and who knows us better than we know ourselves (consider how close He must be!), are eyes which see only the truth; they can see no lie. He cannot see any spell (power) that could bind Israel (ourselves), because <u>He Himself is the Strength and the Deliverer of Israel</u>, the Impenetrable Shield against false divination (the hypnotic spell of anything not God), continually upholding those who are His own.

Yet while Balaam is declaring these very things from the mountain above, in the midst of the camp below, through the hands of angels and mediators, God represents Himself to the children in the wilderness by the law. And make no mistake, it is His law, without any doubt, perfect in every regard, rigid in its standards, and righteous through and through.

So we have to go there, too, to see what this means, so that as we understand the law process happening in us, we may transmit this spiritual rite of passage to others, too, which will go on and on, until ultimately all God's people see the fullness of the glory in which we all already live in Christ.

Law's Dominion – Romans 7:1:

"Know ye not, brethren ... how that the law hath dominion over a man as long as he liveth?" (Rom 7:1. The reader might want to follow along in Romans 7.) The law, meaning in this case life through obedience to outer precepts, concepts, rules, etc., only applies when a man is alive. Only someone alive in himself can hear and respond to the law. The law says, "Thou shalt," and we say, "We will, or at least try." Or the law says, "Thou shalt not," and we say, "We won't, or at least try not to." However, someone who is dead cannot hear the law and therefore cannot respond to it at all.

Paul reinforces that concept in verses 2 and 3, as he then likens our past relationship to the law with that of marriage. He makes the analogy again, that in the death of a spouse we are free from the law of that marriage. Then he explains that, we had been in a marriage relationship with the law, but now if we are dead in Christ's death, as he has declared so plainly in chapter 6, then through the fact of our own death, we are now freed from that past marriage relationship to the law. We are no longer responsible to it. It is as if it no longer exists to us in our death.

Then in verse 4, there is another stunner. Paul says:

"Wherefore, my brethren, ye also are become dead to the law by the body of Christ; that ye should be married to another, even to him who is raised from the dead, that we should bring forth fruit unto God." (Rom 7:4)

Now, this is a strange thing to say for a couple of reasons. One, in chapter 6, he has just told us that we had been the slaves of sin, captives in unrighteousness, or, in effect, married to sin. We had been the wife of sin, bringing forth sin's children.

Now he is telling us we have been the wife of the law, to which we are now dead, in the same way he had just said we were now dead to sin. What gives? How can both be true? This law is God's law, and its commandments are right. Nothing whatsoever is wrong with the law. So why is our marriage to obeying the law described as if it is something to be delivered of or to be dead to, in the same way that death delivers us from our former union with sin and the devil? Satan is not the law, and the law is not Satan. Why is Paul comparing them?

Coming to the Heart

Now we are getting to the heart of the matter, nearer to the goal. We have to remember that we are not trying to come up with some dogmatic way to understand this Romans 7 dilemma and then to apply it, thus "making it work" in our lives. No no no! This is a work of the Spirit, and what we are describing here is that struggle we all face within ourselves that the Holy Spirit works in us to form Christ in us. This is how the Spirit makes real to us the inward truth of who we are in Him and Who He is in us. This bout with the law shows that only He is our living truth, our everything. It is in the turning on of that light of Christ as the only Reality within us, that the lie is dissipated and made null and void. We do not fight the lie, but find and speak the truth, and the lie falls into nothingness. Therefore, what we are unfolding here is what happens as God brings us here. It is God who brings us to this threshold, and Who also takes us to the other side "on wings of eagles."

Paul has said that not only are we dead to the law by the dead body of Jesus Christ, but also by that separation we are now married to Another, Jesus Christ Who is risen. By that marriage to Him, we now bring forth fruit unto God. This is the second strange thing about that verse 4. Because Paul is tying our final freedom, i.e., that of our being able to bring forth fruit unto God, rather than our continual spiritual barrenness, to our freedom from the law. Fruitfulness, Paul is saying, we find linked directly to our death to the law. Now how can that be?

What Paul is saying for those who have ears to hear, is that our, "I want to but can't, or "I don't want to but do," dilemma with sin and life in general, finds it final deliverance in this work of the Spirit and deliverance from the law. The result of deliverance from the law is what we have been looking for for a long time, what any wife looks for. It is the greatest gift of all, that we find ourselves no longer barren, but able to give children to our husband, as Sarah bore Isaac to Abraham, as a child of promise.

This is the discovery we are making: we are finding out how it is we died to the law. Since we have been delivered from the law, by God in Christ, *"blotting out the handwriting of ordinances that was against us, which was contrary to us, and took it out of the way, nailing it to His cross"* (Col 2:14), we now find out how we are now married to Christ, and how that marriage brings forth God's desired children by our lives. This is what Paul is about to tell us.

Verse 5:

Now starting with verse 5, Paul begins to describe how it is the law does this work.

While we were in the flesh – remember our definition from before – the stirrings of sin in us were by the law. What can that mean? How could the law have touched us then when either we were not aware of it or could have cared less? Paul has told us earlier in Romans that we encounter the law two ways. A person born into Israel or into most societies in our time would have been confronted with some degree of a codified divine law from birth. Nevertheless, even those who have no codified law, Paul says, know the law because it is written in our consciences. Therefore, all are without excuse.

So now Paul is saying, even in our former days when we were under the control of Satan, when we lived "according to the prince of the power of the air," sin was stirred up in us by the law, either by codes or by conscience, and the fruit of that stirring, before we were delivered, was death. In other words, we all have always known in the deepest sense what is life and what is death. That is another aspect of the Tree of Knowledge of Good and Evil. Part of its deception is that the knowledge of it does not produce the doing of it. In fact, as we are about to find out, it produces the opposite.

How? How could the law stir up sin? We will defer the question for later, because Paul gets to that. He is just setting the stage right now.

Verse 6:

Paul again states that we are delivered from the law, and the result of that deliverance is that we no longer serve God according to the "letter," but by the "newness" of the Spirit. In other words, we have been delivered from an obedience to a set of laws which were separate from us, which themselves stirred up the sins we were trying to avoid, and now by that deliverance, we live in oneness in a new Spirit (Father, Son, Spirit) within us. We are beginning here to get to the heart of the issue. We are moving from outer to inner, from flesh to Spirit.

Verse 7:

Paul then asks, "Is the law sin?" Of course not, he replies, but it doesn't have the purpose we all thought it did. We all thought the law's purpose was to train us to be godly people. By learning the precepts, commandments, biblical principles and laws, we thought we were taking these things into ourselves and by so doing we would in some way gradually become spiritual people, or at least be somewhat pleasing to God for making the try. It is like teaching a child to brush his teeth in the hopes that it will become habit to him by repetition. However, that is not how things work in the kingdom of God.

We have thought of God's laws and commandments, which are righteous, holy and still viable, as means to an end, to which if we apply ourselves with exceptional diligence, like studying math or grammar, we would someday pass some spiritual exam and become Christ-like. Paul is saying here that the law's purpose is not that at all. No, strangely, the purpose of the law is that we would know sin, not that we would produce righteousness. That seems a strange effect to look for, but it is what Paul has discovered is the purpose of the law.

Verses 8 – 10:

Now the even further result of our bout with attempted obedience to the law, is that we actually find ourselves doing the very things it forbids us. Then Paul gives the example of his own "coveting."

Coveting sounds innocent. It sounds like something innocuous. What is the harm in just "wanting" something? This is not a frivolous issue, however. We are being challenged here to our very inner core. And the issue of "coveting" is at the heart of this matter, because this has to do with what we want, not what we do. This is a much deeper issue that just doing good or bad things.

Paul finds that he cannot control what he desires, and the more he concentrates and strives to avoid having those desires, to not desire, he desires even more. Had the commandment not come, the commandment that says, "Thou shalt not covet," he would not have even been aware that he was in captivity to covetousness. He was living his life, "alive without the law," but unaware of the truth of the matter, which was that he was trapped in an insatiable desire to have for himself. Though he had an outward show of devotion to God, inwardly he discovered that he was driven by a consuming motivation to have what others had and then further, he found himself jealous that they had it and he did not. Then, when his covetousness was pointed out by the law, bringing up in him the desire to escape his possessive coveting, his condition only worsened.

Verses 11 & 12:

"For sin, taking occasion by the commandment, deceived me, and by it slew me." The commandment that says, "Thou shalt not covet," is as right as can be, and points to life, but Paul has found it to be death to him. Why? Sin has used the commandment, the law, Paul says, and by the very law itself, deceived him and by that deception produced death in him. It KILLED him!

How? What is the deception? Here we are getting to the real purpose of the law. <u>The real purpose of the law is to expose the falsely independent self that thinks it can keep the law.</u> The way that God does it is to use the law, which we cannot keep, and Satan as accuser, to remind us continually that in ourselves alone we are hopeless lawbreakers. And then further, because we still think we are in some way capable of obedience, the law, which we think is just "Old Testament" stuff, ramps up a thousand-fold in the New Testament, because the standards in the Old were mostly simple specific deeds and actions. In the New Testament the law (as long as we hear it as "law") unyieldingly demands an impossible obedience to unattainable heights of conduct and love (e.g., "Sermon on the Mount," "Rich young ruler," etc.).

Under the law, whether Old or New, God is always far off from wherever we are. The demands of the New

Testament, under the supposed, "higher law of love," are even more elusive and condemning than Old Testament obedience to precepts in their completion. At least under the Old Testament law, we could keep score, knowing when we had transgressed and when we had not, and we had a remedy. We could perform a sacrifice or a vow, to atone for our infractions. However, the New Testament makes a higher demand – perfection! Moreover, our attempts to become New Testament abiders, New Testament law-keepers, are the same to us in our time as the temple laws were to the Israelites in the time of Jesus. Still, we try, and many of us find that after so much labor we have accomplished very little, and that so much still seems undone, broken and incomplete. We tell ourselves, with others joining in, "Keep trying!" and we do, and *that* is the culprit.

The reason why death occurs when we *try* to keep the law is that the self that thinks it can keep the law, is this same false sin consciousness, i.e., independent, self-relying self. The deception is the deception of sin, of Satan, the originator of this sin and lie, who deceives us that we are capable responsible selves who can keep the law, or in other words, capable in ourselves of our own good or evil. (IF we are originators of our own good or evil, then we are god to ourselves and need no other God!).

He deceived our first parents in the garden by this same deception. He convinced them by their taking and eating the fruit of the Tree of Knowledge of Good and Evil, that they would become wise as gods, and would therefore become equal to God, knowing everything.

That is how sin deceives us when it beats us up with the law. By responding to the commandments as if we could keep them, we are stopped short immediately because we cannot keep them whatsoever. If we keep one, we break another. Therefore, while in this mindset of flesh, of independent self-focus, we cannot help but to buy into the condemnation of the devil, who stands by at the ready to accuse us to ourselves and to God of being perpetual spiritual ne'er do wells, those who are never pleasing to God, ourselves or anyone else. It is this mindset of the flesh, of independent self-focus, of wrongful self-reliance, of separated self, that the law finally exposes for the falsehood and the total fabrication it really is.

Verse 13:
Paul again takes us further into the law's purpose. We see by Paul sharing his actual life struggles with us, that this is not just academic. Nor is he working up a systematic theology that we can all go by for the next two thousand years. Paul is describing what has happened to him in his life with the law, that we might know the same thing when we experience this work of the Spirit, too.

The reason why we fail when we attempt to keep the law through self-effort, is so that this heinous sin which has grasped the whole human race might be exposed in us. It is brought into the light that it might be seen as the heinous sin that it is. This is exceedingly sinful, the abomination of desolation, at least the earnest of it, and it has occurred in every one of us, in that we have all been self-deifiers, little self-gods. We have all lived a life in which we are as a "responsible" self which thinks it generates it own life and in its own will, it sits in the house of God as if it were entitled to the Throne, when it is itself only a caricature of a real person and really nothing but a buffoon. Except that it is not funny in the least, since it is the very heart of sin and wickedness and of every foul thing that ever rebelled against the righteousness of God, and is the house of the devil.

That is the purpose of the law – to show us that creature in our very selves that has tainted all that we are, the devil-infected creature of self-focused, "I, me, mine" – and then through the law's work of killing "us" by this exposure, we might know our total and final deliverance from this snake and his lies.

Verse 14:

Here Paul makes the classic statement, one of the most argued over and misunderstood phrases in scripture: *"I am carnal, sold under sin."*

We see here that Paul is speaking metaphorically, as if he is just flesh, that he is just the old person he used to be. He is speaking autobiographically I am certain, but I am equally certain he is not talking about his current daily life in the Spirit. If he is, then we should cut out the sixth chapter of Romans before and the eighth chapter after this, and while we're at it let's throw out Galatians, Ephesians, Colossians, Philippians, and the book of Hebrews, too. The message that we are just hopeless sinners and remain so is not the message of the New Testament and is not the truth for those born again in Jesus Christ!

Paul is only using a figure of speech when he says he is carnal, sold under sin. That is part of the deception of sin: that we are enslaved to it, and we cannot help our involvement in it. If we say that we are still slaves to sin and cannot do anything but continue in it, we are also saying we are still slaves of the devil and the Cross has no effect! That is just what Paul has taken all this time in the previous chapters of his Romans letter to refute. In Romans 6 in the strongest of terms, using plain words without ambiguous meaning, Paul declared that we are no longer slaves of sin, and now that we are no longer slaves to sin, we therefore have no more debt to it, to obey it "in our members."

"How shall we, who are DEAD TO SIN, live any longer therein?" Paul asks as a challenge in Romans 6:2. Surely he does not answer his own question with a sad, "Oh well, we still have to live in sin every day even though we are dead to it." What kind of crazy logic would that be? As I said, the whole theme of the 6th chapter of Romans is precisely that we ARE NO LONGER slaves of sin, that now in being raised to "newness of life," the "members" of our humanity – spirit, soul and body – are now the servants, slaves, and bearers of righteousness.

Therefore, Paul is speaking metaphorically of a past struggle here, when he says he is carnal, sold under sin. Everything about Paul's life, ministry, and writings dispel the notion that Paul still walks around in a state of continual sinning. *"Out of them all the Lord delivered me,"* Paul wrote to Timothy. He is the one who worked *"more mightily than they all."* Paul's life does not speak of continual effort and continual defeat, but only of victory, only of glory, only of the stuff of Joshua and Caleb – faith.

What he is describing is the process by which that struggle is finished in us, through which we come into God's rest in our inner selves. The Spirit opens our understanding so that we begin to know inwardly that

His yoke is easy, that His burden is light, and that His righteousness, expressed in our daily living in thought, word, and deed, comes through grace by means of His Spirit life in us, as we will come to in the next chapter of Romans.

But first we have to see how the Law has its perfect work in us, as Paul continues in the next few verses of Romans 7.

Verses 15 – 20:

Paul now comes to his famous lament, repeated in prayers every day in every nation, by men and women everywhere, in church or out. We prayed Paul's predicament every time we had communion in my former church. It was honest as far as we knew, and heartfelt. Certainly that is how life feels, the older we grow and the more experience we have. "We have done those things which we ought not to have done, and have left undone those things which we ought to have done," we prayed every Sunday, and I think everybody earnestly meant it. Somehow in that confession we felt relieved for a little while, at or least forgiven for that moment in the bread and wine, the prayers and the absolution. And certainly I am not discounting that grace was there, for it was there for me.

However, instead of accepting that predicament as a lifelong situation, Paul is driven onward. He does not camp out in his despair but keeps pressing on. He starts questioning himself and this whole process. What is going on here, he wonders. What about the law? I know that to keep the commandments is good, he says. God's laws, His standards, are right. And I know that and believe that, and want it to be true in my life. And because I inwardly want this to be so, that I don't want to be a lawbreaker, that I want to keep God's law, I have come to realize that something outside of me, something that is not me, i.e., something not the real me, is making this happen. What is doing this?

His conclusion is that the problem is something he calls "sin." And he says it dwells in him, "in me." So anything dwelling "in me" makes it very intimate, but there is also a sense about his description of this indweller that makes it foreign to Paul, something he recognizes as an invader with some sort of toehold, but not really part of him.

Let us stop here for a moment. Paul says, *"<u>sin</u> that dwelleth <u>in</u> me."* Those are strong words. There can be no mistake, this is not the confession of someone living in the self-lust of the prince of the power of the air. *"I delight in the law of God after the inward man,"* can only be the cry of the Spirit of God, speaking in Paul's mouth. Therefore, this is an already redeemed Paul speaking of his own final confrontation with the law.

So our first question has to be, what is this sin he is speaking of? Then our next one follows: then how can it be living in me?

We have previously identified sin, not to be an abstract principle, but as a person. Above we have gone over the scriptural basis on which we say that sin is a person, to which we will add this. The reason we say sin is a person, rather than a principle or a law, is because at the bottom of all things, there are no separate "principles" or "laws" floating around the universe. There is only One Person at the bottom of everything, "the ground of all being," as Paul Tillich calls God. Everything comes out of "person."

But there is a furtherance of that person-life out of God into His creation, and we are those created persons, something we share in part in common with angels. In being persons, we are privileged to be distinct in ourselves as "I am," yet deriving our "I am" from He Who is the Only True, "I AM THAT I AM." We find our right selves only in Him, existing as expressions and manifestors of Him.

But in that we are truly persons, created in His image, we are also participators in the expansion and development of His creation. His purpose is that we as creatures might fully participate in His eternal creation, manifesting the Life of God through our created lives, expanding the Word and God's kingdom through the forms that God expresses in our lives. And this is to the heart of the matter, because in Lucifer, whose knowledge of the power of creation sought to rival the Father's, that self fire we have been speaking of, again strove almost infinitely for itself, and birthed a separate will, a will that sought to overcome God by being like God, which is sin and became hell. Prior to Lucifer's rebellion, there had been no "sin principle." He was the originator, or as Jesus called him, "the father of lies." That is the sense in which we say sin is not a principle, but is a person. Even as we say God is Love, not God "has" love, in the same way we say Lucifer IS sin, and any participation in sin, is not just participating in a principle, but in the person whose principle it is.

God Means It for Good

However, we do not have this knowledge so we can wring our hands and fret and say how sorry we are it has come to this. There is a joke being played on us here!

Because in wreaking his evil havoc Satan is only as Joseph's brothers who also meant what they did to Joseph for evil. They were God's servants in their evil, because it was God's purpose that the sons of Jacob threw Joseph into a pit. It was God's pleasure that they sold him to traveling Ishmaelites (their cousins) going down to Egypt. God designed Joseph's post as Potiphar's steward, knowing it would lead to his downfall and imprisonment. Joseph had to face the temptress and prevail, even though he was falsely accused and then thrown into prison to languish for years. It pleased the Lord to bruise Joseph for His purposes. (Is 53:10), and this was God's joy. It was God's unabashed delight that Pharaoh raised Joseph to second in the kingdom, (as a man in Christ becomes king over all God's works in his life, second only to God, having become servant to all).

But then it was shown to be God's purpose all along, when his brothers showed up from Canaan in the famine, bowing to him as foretold in the dream which had caused their jealousy so long before, that he might be a refuge for his father at the end of his life. In the same way, our Christ is a refuge for His Father in that He has brought many sons unto Him and delivers unto Him the kingdom in the end. Moreover, all of this, from the pit to the throne, was God's purposed plan, *"to save much people alive."* (Gen 50:20) Let the devil have his purposes and works of evil from morning until night, because we KNOW that each and every one of them are meant by God for good and to "save much people alive," without exception!

Still, it can be disturbing that Paul says that his problem is sin dwelling <u>in</u> him. We have just identified sin as a person, and that person is the creator or originator of sin, Satan. Are we then to conclude that after we have been delivered from sin and Satan as our inner death and condemnation, after Jesus has cast him out in the Cross, that he has regained entry into us somehow?

No, of course not! Through the Cross Satan has been put out of us, spirit, soul and body, and the One who effected our rescue, stands guard to prevent Satan's retaking us. He is "ever living," Hebrews says, "to make intercession for us." (Heb 7:25). Abiding in the Son, we have come to total safety and refuge in God. He promises no one can pluck us out of His hand, and we know that He speaks the truth. Understand, when Paul is talking about sin dwelling "in me," and again, "in my flesh," he is talking about our flesh-consciousness. He has correctly identified his problem is not his intrinsic self. Nor can it be simply his body, as we have mentioned before.

"I know that in me (that is, in my flesh,) dwelleth no good thing: for to will is present with me ..." He is now seeing his emptiness, his "not good-ness." He has not found evil in his purpose and desire, so that is not the problem. Now he is realizing that this "arm of the flesh" that he has been exercising all his life, his own self-reliance, his own self-responsibility, is simply nothing. It is "no good thing." All his self-strivings emanate from absolutely nothing. First, they are not even necessary. Moreover, they do or accomplish nothing. They are only a smokescreen or a veil in front of the truth of who we already are without those self-strivings.

Paul finds ultimately that he can only be, at rock bottom, an emptiness, a poverty of spirit, at the heart of which is the will to life, but in his newly-discovered poverty and emptiness he lacks the means to bring about his will – to bring forth "fruit unto God." In his deepest heart, he wills God's will, and by that willing, Paul is brought to this point – and so are we!

Verse 21:

Now Paul is reaching the end of himself and the final key to this dilemma. He says that he finds it a law, in other words, this is the way it works and now I am seeing how it works. How it works is this. When "I" – and here he is meaning himself in a mindset of separation, of false self-responsibility and effort – would do good, or try to do good, evil is present.

We are so geared to thinking deeds; it is easy to miss this. He does not say that he does something evil, though in the preceding verses he had said he is unable to figure out how to perform the good he wants to do, and that the evil he wants not to do, he finds himself doing. He does not repeat that here. Instead, Paul says, "when I would do good, evil is present with me."

This is something deeper. Evil is present, he is saying, in the "I would." The very reach into, "<u>I will try</u> to be like God," (be Christlike) is the most subtle temptation there is, because it sounds so righteous and holy, and there is no one on earth who has not fallen to it. That is what the law has finally gouged out of Paul (<u>and now out of us</u>)! He is touched here to his deepest core, and now in absolute honesty he is seeing the hiding place, the lair of the culprit.

Christ has cast out the pretender, but as a disgruntled fired programmer might plant a worm or a virus in the company computer before he leaves, so that from offsite he can continue to have access, that evil bad devil left that mindset when he left us. God let him leave it, even though it is a mindset that still is Satan's to manipulate (of course, nothing really is "his"). It was left with good reason, because it is this mindset of independence, self-effort, i.e., the flesh consciousness, <u>that God uses to bring us to this point</u>. God wastes nothing, and all the events of our lives – positives and negatives – He perfectly works according to His purposes (Eph 1:11)! We see this as God's process, through and through, not something engineered by Satan to trip us up. This is the necessary school the Spirit puts us through that we might grow up into Him in all things. And He means us to get thrashed, thrashed and thrashed some more, until all the stuffing of self-righteousness we tried to fill ourselves in with, is cast off forever into the dust heap, and we finally find His fullness in our complete and utter abandoned emptiness!

Verses 22 – 23:

As we said above, we delight in God from our inward heart. Through and through we are billowed over by Him in absolute rapture. Despite these struggles, despite the agony, still every day He has shown Himself to be our only love and life, and nothing can shake us from Him.

Nevertheless, Paul is disturbed about this. He is not settling for this struggle as something permanent. He is about to crack up with it, and just the knowledge that when he tries to do good, evil is present with him, is no solution in itself, though at last he realizes that his own self-efforts accomplish nothing for him, and that is the beginning of the revelation of all revelations. He is coming to the end of "himself," i.e., his own self-efforts, self-responsibility, and self-ability. He has finally come to see, in a final sense – "I can't do this."

He has correctly identified his inner self as righteous (through Christ in him), as he stated clearly in chapter 6. But this other thing, in his "members," "in me," "in my flesh" as he variously describes the same reality – flesh consciousness in separation, self-reliance, wrongful self-focus, etc. – is driving him crazy because he cannot go on like two people in one body, as if one side of him serves sin and the other side serves righteousness. He preaches the exact opposite of that, so either what he has been telling people is wrong, or there has to be a solution beyond perpetual spiritual hell!

Whatever happened to, *"But whosoever drinketh of the water that I shall give him shall never thirst"*? (John 4:14) Is there no rest in God? O God, where did you go? Restore unto me the joy of thy salvation! O **_WRETCHED_** man that I am!!!

Verse 24:

And there we are. We finally come to the bottom when we have no more to give or anywhere to go. We have emptied out; there is nothing left, and what there was was not enough anyway. Our cruse of oil has run out. All our righteousness really is like filthy rags and now we know it. We still thought we had a rag or two He would accept. Or maybe we thought He might not notice when we substituted our own self rags for the proper wedding garments only He gives. When He said, "Love others," we tried to and thought that was enough. Didn't He notice how hard we tried? He said, "Be humble," and we studied humility so we could be more humble than anybody else. But He noticed, and said, *"NO FLESH SHALL ENTER MY PRESENCE!."*

So now we have finally seen it, that sin is exceedingly sinful. God in His perfect love will have nothing but truth, righteousness and holiness in us, all of which come <u>only</u> from Him. There is no other truth, no other righteousness, no other holiness, except He Himself. We cannot assert some false truth, false righteousness, or false holiness that we make up ourselves to offer up to Him. They are the palest of imitations and have the consistency of smoke in the wind. Once we've seen it for ourselves, this self-reliant self that thinks it is something when it is nothing (Gal 6:3), then by the Spirit's revelation we know it is an abomination, and becomes to us forever the accursed thing, and we never want to touch it again.

We have seen this monumentally earthshaking thing, that while in this consciousness of flesh I am in a body of death, and I cannot help myself in my participation in it, (i.e., I can't believe right, think right, act right, know right or do anything else right as some self "technique" I can use to rescue or keep myself). And it is at this point from which we finally call out for rescue from this perpetual wheel of hell in the greatest desperation ever, a call to someone to PLEASE COME and save my life! ***"Who shall deliver me?"***

This is not academic. One does not come here except God brings him here. Because this is rock bottom. We all have a built-in resistance to rock bottom, so we may swirl around the drain for a long time. But eventually we let go of the side and go down the drain. Here one cannot go on any further. God had better come through or else.

Or not. For me at that point, when I said to God, "I quit, I can't keep myself. If it's going to be done you'll have to do it, because I can't. I QUIT!" I meant it. I had truly come to the end. I knew I had no more strength to go on in God's life. I could not make the next hurdle. In utter desperation I said, "I quit, you do it!" and then lay down and in effect, died.

So this is LIFE, not a concept or principle Paul is calling for. He is not even quoting a scripture and standing on it. He is calling for HELP! WHO CAN HELP ME? WHO? WHO? He is calling for **A SOMEBODY**!

Verse 25:

"I thank God through Jesus Christ our Lord ..." Now Paul's deliverance from the law, and thus finally from all the ruin of the enemy's lie which is undone forever in this moment of light and revelation, is coming into full view.

The first tremendous thing Paul is seeing is that in his own just discovered "nothingness," Another, Jesus Christ the Lord, has come right into this spot, into this nothingness and filled it with Himself. He has come here just as He has come all our lives in all the other spots. <u>He is</u> the Deliverer. <u>He is</u> the sword, shield and buckler. <u>He is</u> the one to overcome this seemingly impossible dilemma. <u>He is</u> the One, by His own life in us AS us, Who will bring us Himself into the land of His abundance. <u>He is</u> the fulfiller of all the "Thou shalts."

Then Paul has seen this principle to the uttermost, when he says, "with the mind I serve the law of God, and with the flesh the law of sin." Again, he is talking of consciousness. One is consciousness of the Spirit – a mind set on the Spirit he says later in the next chapter, and the other a mind set on the flesh. It is not two minds existing at once, constantly warring each other and canceling each other out, though for a time it appears like that.

This cannot possibly be a giving over of humanity back to the helplessness of sin, so that we must, as one lady said in a meeting recently, inevitably sin. Paul has just been given a revelation of the final depths to our salvation, in the revelation of flesh and spirit, in that they are not warring parties each contending to win out in us, but wholly separate realities, both in God's being, but one true and one false. Paul is simply saying that one mind, the mind of the Spirit, is the reality of Life outgoing, of love expressing righteousness and holiness in flesh (earthen) containers. And that the other mind, the mind (consciousness) of the flesh, which we have described over and over above, is the false reality of independent "me" orientation, which is death, and produces the fruit of death.

No Condemnation – Romans 8:1

In Romans 8:1, Paul reaches critical mass. This little, innocuous, so often used term, "no condemnation," is like the sudden great flash of light that precedes everything else in a nuclear detonation. Suddenly there is Light, brighter than a million noonday suns. Only Light and nothing else. Then comes Sound and Wind, out of a center of Fire.

Like that nuclear explosion, "no condemnation" is pure and is an explosion of grace, a flash right out of the depths of Heaven, enlightening the very landscape of all existence with God Who is Truth. In a flash, the Spirit opens our understanding to see that nothing in us, nothing we are, nothing we have done or are doing now, is under any condemnation from Him in this present moment. There is no condemnation in Him and we are in Him. We have this assurance from the Highest Authority and Judge in the Universe, the Lord Jesus Christ who said and says, "Neither do I condemn thee ... Go and sin no more!" (And even the commandment to "sin no more," has no further sting to it, because we know He is the fulfiller of His own word, which <u>He promises</u> will bear fruit in us.)

Each one of us in some degree knows or has known this condemnation. This is far more than some psychological guilt complex. It is not a "Christian" negative self-image. This condemnation is from deeper sources than our own psychology or past behaviors. It has nothing to do with anything about ourselves as we might think. It has nothing to do, for instance, with whether I am a confident person or a timid person. One knows this spiritual condemnation as much as another does.

Likewise, we are not more condemned for bad behavior or less condemned for good behavior. All of us share it, because we have been born into the inheritance of Adam: *"Therefore as by the offence of one judgment came upon all men to condemnation..."* Rom 5:18a

The choice in the Garden was not about judging between good and evil, or right and wrong. That is what the whole world lives in, but judging good and evil was not the choice. It was about living out of life or out of death. When they took the fruit, which they thought would make them "wise as gods," they chose death (having been warned beforehand), and condemnation immediately appeared on the scene – and has hounded our heels ever since. It is like a sense of impending doom that says we must hide, protect, hunker down, make boundaries, declare territories, to cringe, to attack, to do anything to ward off certain death as long as is possible.

Now this condemnation, which means a continual sentence of death hanging over our heads, is the natural outcome of living by the law, of living by "knowing good and evil." The law as outer precepts is impersonal. It has no mercy or grace. Its breaking contains an immediate sentence of death that has no remedy. And since we have all broken it, we all experience the rightful condemnation which comes from the law. It is continuous and lasts as long as we are subject to the law.

That is what happened with Adam and Eve (and also with us). The tempter convinced them that they were incomplete as they were, and needed something more than God had already given them in order to complete themselves, to become "wise as gods." But as soon as they partook of the Tree of the Knowledge of Good and Evil, the self-knowledge they sought instantly became in them fear and death – condemnation!

However, we have learned that now in the Cross we have been delivered from the law, and therefore released from the condemnation coming from it. Romans 7 is about finding out that we cannot approach God by that path. The reason we cannot approach God down this road is that the law, though both inwardly and outwardly representative of Him, still is, in a sense, "one step removed" from God. It is not He Himself. The Law expresses the nature of God, yet it is not God. There simply is no set of standards that anyone could write, much less apply and obey, that could possibly elevate the created onto an equal par with the Creator.

Paul said the law *"was ordained by angels in the hand of a mediator. Now a mediator is not a mediator of one, but God is one."* (Gal 3:19, 20) In other words, the law is separation. Under the law, we are one-step removed from God and always remain so. The veil that divides us (condemnation – Gen 3:6-10) continually remains. The veil is there because of the law and the flesh (independent self-mindedness) that tries to keep the law.

Living by the Law is Separation

The law presupposes the separate self to obey it. The fact that we see the law outside us as something we have to attain to, something which we are not now but should or ought to be, is our perpetual admission that we are lawbreakers and in separation from God. In this separation, we can only hear the law as if it is coming from outside us and therefore we are apart from it, so that we are bound to both the demands of the law and to the separateness in which to do them.

This separate outer law demands that we live up to the reality that we are the image of God. That is an impossibility, because we are only an image, and not God Himself. Only God can be God. An image does not create or sustain itself, but is dependent on the object of which it is an image. We are images that have come out of the breath of God, and so we have some measure of life and will in ourselves – for we are <u>persons</u> in His image! As persons, we have all been tempted to try to become God ourselves by trying to be like Him, whether knowingly or unknowingly. It is the most absurd thought that ever came into the temporal universe. Still, we have all tried it. Like Lucifer, we have all said, "I will be like the Most High." (Is 14:14).

Nevertheless, the very attempt to emulate God, even if out of a supposed good motive – to do "good" – is the point of separation from God, because no separate will can work in Him. A will that says, "I will be like Him," is already separated unto itself and not to God, because no created being can be like Him. He is Himself and there is no other. However, He has created us that through Christ in us we would be the visible expression of which He is the invisible reality, so that our lives are what they are supposed to be when we are one with God. Something that is one with something has no need to become or change into something else – to "be like" something, because it already IS a perfect expression of that with which it is "one." It just is itself, and thinks and wills as one with its source. As a branch of a vine lives only from the sap from the vine, and therefore bears the fruit of the vine through its organic oneness with the vine, in the same exact way we bear the fruit of Christ since we are one with Him and are living branches on His vine.

What happens as we discover our release by death from this false self-relying self, this false "I" that set itself up as God within us, is that we are overtaken by a new reality. We realize that through baptism into Him we have gone into His death and our old self – whatever it was – has died. It is a new self that rises in His resurrection, a self that is not just me alone trying to do God's will or to resist the devil. He has come into me to be one person with me! There is a new "I" – a new identity – a new person, consisting of an organic union where two have become one. I do not become "like" Him, but instead He has come to live in "me" to be the "real me," and in "you" to be the "real you." He and I live as one person together in spirit and function. (1 Cor 6:17).

This is where our NO condemnation takes form in us. We have grown up all our lives knowing nothing but this condemnation. If others did not put it on us then we put it on ourselves. We know our guilt, we know what we deserve, and now this Romans 7 has brought it all sharply into focus.

However, here we find Paul at the end of Romans 7, finally coming to the resolution of his struggle, like a slow train, steadily getting there. He has now taken us to the final hump, where he sees two operations, one the law of sin and death, or the law of the flesh, and the other the law of the spirit of life in Christ Jesus.

This is an important juncture here, and the absolute crux of the matter. On one hand Paul seems to be saying that he is operating both laws simultaneously, walking in his flesh according to the flesh, and at the same time in his spirit walking according to the Spirit. That cannot be our solution!

Or on the other hand, Paul seems to be saying that he walks one way one moment – when he minds the flesh he walks according to the flesh – and another way another moment – when he minds the Spirit he walks according to the Spirit. *This is the answer, after all that groaning? What madness is that?* Do we accept ourselves now as *Dr. Jekyll and Mr. Hyde?* Are we still left with some wild animal in us still chained up, that is always wanting to escape and every once in a while, to our great chagrin, despite all our efforts to keep him at bay, jumps the fence with his fangs bared and his hair on end? Is there NO END to this?

We seem to be left there holding just that bag as we close out Romans 7.

The problem seems to be at this point, if we were left just here, is that the solution is a sort of limbo, and the limbo is because we don't really know which way this is going to go. However, this limbo is really the final nail in the coffin of this self that thinks it is something in itself and has some capability now to operate the life of the Spirit. Who is sufficient for these things?

The vast majority of the Church of Christ through the centuries has been stuck right here in this limbo. We cannot keep ourselves from sin, and cannot propel ourselves into the fullness of spiritual life. The reason why things are stuck at this point is that this is the limit of what we might call doctrine or teaching, or conceptual knowledge. For 1500 years the church has put most of its eggs in that basket. The basket of right doctrine. Which will get us quite a way. It is a good thing to seek the truth and to understand it.

Nevertheless, this is the point through which concepts cannot carry us. Nor can slogans, or standing on scriptures, or words of faith, or anything else we might conceive of. That is why this is a limbo. We may try to fill the limbo with a doctrine of what happens next or what the flesh/spirit war is and how we fight it, but the fact is the words of Paul give us no clear answer and leave us hanging! Except where it points us to and leaves us to the Spirit. Only the Spirit, by a sheer miracle, can pull/push us through the eye of this needle!

Knowing the concepts in this book will not do it. Taking a class teaching these things will not cause us to learn it. Applying the principles taught in a class will not make it happen.

The reason is this: What the Lord is bringing out of us is His true and actual life, manifested in spirit and truth in our mortal flesh. Therefore, it can only come from Him in grace and truth. It must be grace because it is an understatement to say we could produce in any measure in ourselves the outgoing grace of God. Grace is not only received, but is transmitted, and we can only transmit what we receive. Our commission is to transmit God in His grace, which we find impossible to do in ourselves, and yet it MUST be. It MUST be grace flowing out, but only God can dispense the true grace. It is not by clever words or the accuracy of our doctrines that we can fulfill this commission, so we find ourselves on our faces in our hearts, and losing ourselves in trusting Him to be the grace that He is – in us!

In addition, it must be truth because if it is not truth then it is not God. But we cannot confuse truth with concepts. When we seek God only, then God only will satisfy and anything less is misery. Therefore if the Lord is to bring out anything real in us, it must truly be God who does it, not just we parroting words, doctrines or truths we have heard. We are only satisfied with the outflow of the True Living God on whom we have latched with our whole hearts. By sheer grace He has caused us to hang on through thick or thin, even when we couldn't hold on and gave up on believing, all the while knowing we are sunk if God does not come through, because we have nowhere left to go.

Because now we have realized this tremendous, earthshaking news about ourselves, that we cannot do anything of ourselves! We are dead, and <u>dead people do not try</u>! When we finally know the "arm of the flesh" is of no use, then we see that only a rescue from outside can get us out of this quicksand, and the Rescuer is HERE.

It is like light directly from heaven to see we are nothing in ourselves, and to see from an observer's point of view, opening in our consciousness by the Spirit, how with the flesh we walk in the law of sin and death, and with the "mind", we walk according to the Spirit of life in Christ Jesus. O how wonderful! Praise God, that is how it is, and now we see it!

Twoness Supplanted by Oneness

But wait! What's next? There must be more to this than knowing that fact, glorious as that is. Unless something further comes, in which this continual inescapable twoness (between God and myself and between myself and myself) is supplanted by a certain wholeness and eternal (continuous) oneness, I'm still stuck, because what I have learned through this valley of self-effort the Lord has taken me through, is that I can do nothing of myself. Therefore I cannot of myself operate the life of the Spirit, nor keep myself in it. No, not ever!

The conscious life of the Spirit begins when the Spirit opens our consciousness to the fact that it is forever, "Not I, but He," and, "the Son can do nothing of Himself … the Father that dwells in me, He does the works!"

The Spirit always operates the life of the Spirit, so that we are forever in weakness as the lambs of God. This is our final hump. On one side it perpetually appears as if we are two, sometimes flesh and sometimes spirit. But when we come through this portal onto the other side, where we know Christ and ourselves joined as one spirit (Holy Spirit joined to human spirit to make one spirit, 1 Cor 6:17), we know the Life we are now living is Christ, and that He has now appeared by His Spirit here in our form (mortal flesh – 2 Cor 4:11) to be in us our All in the alls there are.

What is different?

What is different? Maybe not much. Paul's problem of "coveting" was perhaps only noticeable to him as an inner struggle, so little may have changed in one sense, in the sense that Paul's human life went on as before. He never says he quit coveting, only that no condemnation came and then after that he saw himself caught up in and walking in the Spirit. He finds new uses for his humanity that had seemed ready for the discard heap. He never mentions his possessive coveting again, but again and again Paul expresses "coveting" for other things – the salvation of his brethren the Jews, to preach the gospel where it has not been preached before, to continue to reach for the prize, which was not just his own personal resurrection, but the prize of being in on the resurrection of others to newness of life. He covets more than anything to plant the plants God covets, and spends everything in his life for that end. "Spending and being spent." (2 Cor 12:15).

Paul does not speak a further word about personal problems with sin. He does not say he never sins again; he just does not mention it anymore. After all that desperation and anguish, Paul expresses no further concern about himself or his motivations. He is no longer that self preoccupied with itself as in Romans 7. In another place, he says he no longer judges himself, having entrusted all self-judgment to the Lord and the Spirit. His self-oriented concern about personal behavior, whether outwardly or inwardly, becomes in the Spirit an outgoing concern geared to one purpose, to give his all that others might find life. Everything Paul talked about after this was about God being the sufficiency and power in everything and every instance of life. As he also said, "to live is Christ." (Phil 1:21).

Certainly, a change does occur, but it is a change in consciousness, from flesh to spirit, making everything new. We have finally left the separation of the law, i.e., knowing "about" God, as if God is an object we could study, analyze and "become like." Now having gone over this hump, we come into <u>knowing God</u>, not as an "over there" person we can look at and touch, but as being mixed in union and oneness in that union through Jesus, so that inwardly we now know that we living are He living. One person expressing Himself as the Same Person in many sons.

All our lives God has spoken to us and in us in various ways, drawing us to Himself in order to reveal the Son in us. Every moment God has been saying in all our hearts, "You are my beloved son," even if for long years we could not hear His voice. All that time the Father has perfectly been drawing us into Him, little by little, in every circumstance and event of our lives, in order to reveal His love and His Son – in us!

Now here, as we are coming into a life that is the literal and substantial life of Christ living out and expressed in the world through and AS our humanity, a tremendous shockwave hits our mortality, swallowing it up into life. For the first time we hear in ourselves God speaking, "You are released from death, and have passed forever into my Life. You may rest from your labors in Me, knowing that I AM the Life in you. Go your way; I do not condemn you!"

Suddenly everything in the universe turns around and changes. The music changes keys. Dissonance that has been there so long it is almost unnoticed suddenly becomes harmony and we notice!

We have found favor! There is One Who sees us as we are and delights in us as we are!

"How could that be for one such as me?" we ask. Only God knows, but here we are – now delivered from the law; now delivered from the self-efforts of a falsely independent self and all its tricks and foibles; now delivered by great wonders out of darkness into light. Right now here we are, called and chosen of God, to bear His name and light in fear and trembling into the world.

The handwriting of ordinances – the law – which rightly testified against us, God removed, nailing it to Jesus' cross, where Christ bore it Himself (Col 2:14). And the inner dread, the condemnation it brought us all our lives is pierced through with that same nail, and borne by Him as well.

The word of NO condemnation is the portal, the announcement, of that which is to come, because condemnation is that last little bit that has been about "me," and from now on, we move away from "me" in the life of the Spirit. As we become settled in who we are – Christ living as us – we move into an entirely "for others" life, out of the spontaneity of the Spirit who is working all God's purposes perfectly in every circumstance and event in our lives. We no longer accept the devil's condemnation because we are Christ living as us, and are therefore the "beloved Son," in Whom the Father is always pleased. Having passed out of the inheritance of Adam into the inheritance of Christ, we are no longer of the kingdom of condemnation, and gladly bid it farewell.

The Law of the Spirit of Life: Romans 8:2

Now, as we said before, we move immediately away from ourselves, and begin to see what has happened as we come through into this fullness of God.

Paul takes us right into the total, as he describes how this new law has taken over, the "law of the spirit of life in Christ Jesus," and how that law, which we now find operative in us, has accomplished a final release from the former law under which we were held – the "law of sin and death."

For our purposes, we are dealing with two definitions of law. One definition is simply the natural way by which something works. We call what happens when we let go of an object and it falls to the ground, an example of the law of gravity. In this case, the law of gravity is not some outside separate influence on matter, telling it that it must fall if it is released. The law of gravity is instead the description of how things function normally in this universe.

If I hold a rock up chest high and then let it go, it would immediately fall to the ground. The rock would function according to the natural law of what it is, a rock, and would be automatically attracted to the earth by its irresistible gravitational force. That is an example of a naturally functioning law.

There are no written instructions for the rock to refer to, nor does anyone have to tell the rock to fall. It just does because it is natural to it. It would be silly to tell the rock it should or ought to fall. Let it go and it falls, without instruction or extra encouragement. This is something working according to the natural law of what it is.

The other use of "law" has to do with codes and admonitions that outwardly tell us how things should or ought to work. Elsewhere Paul has told us this outer set of codes and precepts regarding human behavior, called "the law," are not for the righteous, but for the unrighteous. In the beginning there was no law contained in precepts. It only entered the picture when disobedience and unbelief came on the scene. Going back to our law of gravity picture, if we were to let go of the rock and instead of falling down it were to fall up, *then* it would be necessary to apply an outer law to remind or even force the rock to keep its own inner law.

That is what has happened now that unbelief has entered the picture. We have been taken captive by another law through the spirit of error, using the knowledge of good and evil as the instrument and implementer of the law of sin and death. Through that captivity, we no longer function naturally according to the inner law out of which our being is compounded, the law of self-giving love – which is really not a law, but is the image of God with which we are all stamped and in whose single existence [being] we find our own existence.

We are still functioning in love, but it is love in malfunction, because that love has been captured and turned inward on ourselves. God mercifully then sends the law of precepts and codes to us, which, since we are caught in the Tree of the Knowledge of Good and Evil, makes some sense to us because we know we should be "good" and we each know secretly our own "evil." Therefore, it strikes home.

God then uses this law of precepts variously in our lives to bring us one way or another to full acknowledgement of our deep selfishness in thought, word, and deed, and then finally the same law of precepts brings us to this current threshold. This is where by the Spirit we have seen the breaking of this lifelong consciousness of a self spiritually deluded into a consciousness of false independence, which has manifested all our lives as self-righteousness, self-effort, self-responsibility, self-pity, self-depreciation, etc. This is Satan's secret hiding place, and is the absolute core, rock bottom, where the ***axe is laid to the root of the tree***. Satan's whole lie, which has entangled us all our lives, has had its secret hiding place the whole of our lives right here at this root of false independent self. Now through exposure to the light, the root is gone, and there is no more hidey-hole in us for him to hide in. From now on he may holler at us from over the fence or off the path, but the light has finally exposed the real truth that we are one with Christ, and no lie stands a chance in that light.

Now we have come to the "end of ourselves." We have come firmly to see by the Spirit's revelation that we died with Him in His cross; we were crucified with Him, dying with Him to the satanic spirit of sin who held us captive. Now by virtue of His death and resurrection comes this inner word of revelation to us, by which we now *know* we are dead to the law, dead to sin and Satan, and, being dead, we again now *know* to the uttermost we can do nothing of ourselves, because dead people cannot do anything at all.

What is the law of the Spirit of life?

> *The wind bloweth where it listeth, and thou hearest the sound thereof, but canst not tell whence it cometh, and whither it goeth: so is every one that is born of the Spirit. (John 3:8)*

The "death" we have experienced in coming to the end of ourselves, in "forsaking all that we have" (how much more complete can death be?) is now the open door for the floodwaters of the Spirit. Though the Spirit has been there all along, as long as we were full in ourselves, we could not recognize Him. It is only in our continual human emptiness that we find the fullness of the Godhead bodily living in us as us.

The reason why everything changes at this point is that we have changed our focus. The law only operates in separation. We have viewed the self (ourselves) as if we were separate from God and therefore we are supposed to add something more to the work God has already accomplished. However, the Spirit is continually saying inwardly in the self, "Be still, and know that I AM God." But the law says the opposite of, "Be still." Instead, the law, speaking to us as if we are alive and separate, says, "YOU must get up and do, accomplish, fulfill, obey, resist …" And in that separated consciousness, we try to comply, which is all we know to do, since from birth the focus of our spiritual sight has not been God in ourselves, but on ourselves as if we are alone and everything is up to what WE do about ourselves. It is all about us and nothing whatsoever we can do will rescue us from that self-focus.

Now in this death, this consciousness of a falsely independent, self-relying self, on whom we had focused so long, has died. The self that tries to obey the law has died. Its death has been its exposure for what it is in plain light: a complete falsehood, a lie told by the devil, which we have believed and made the whole basis for our whole lives, making this lie the center out of which everything we have ever thought or done has come. But now in this moment of light, which is also utter truth, behold, it is NOTHING, as is the liar who fabricated it, and it falls to the ground with no life in it.

This death makes way for the new self that now stands up, visible in the eyes of the Spirit. The new self has only one awareness, "I live, yet not I, but Christ liveth," and has only one food and delight, "Lo, I come to do thy will, O God."

Now the focus of our knowledge and understanding has been "taken up" into a higher truth, a greater reality, where God reveals Himself as the hidden propagator in everything. This new self that rises up as us, God takes up into the rapture of the Spirit, because its life pours out of One Who is everywhere present in all things.

The law of the Spirit of life in Christ Jesus is simply this revelation having come into fullness in us: *"And this is life eternal, that they might know Thee the only true God, and Jesus Christ, whom thou hast sent."* (John 17:3)

The law of the Spirit of life in Christ Jesus is being taken up into the knowing of God. Here we leave truth "about." True "knowing" is not conceptual knowledge. It is not the accumulation of facts and evidences. It may start there, but if it stays there, it is trapped in it.

Knowing Is Being

True knowing is being. One becomes, or is, that which he knows. That is why Jesus said, "Ye shall know them by their fruit." One is known by what he is, and one is what one knows.

For instance, if one truly knows truth, he is truth. It is not because he has learned facts about what truth is, or that he has practiced them. It is because to know truth is to be truth. One cannot speak or be what he does not know, because it is not familiar to him. Nevertheless, if you know truth, then truth is what you are, what you do, what you say. There is no separation between you and truth, as if truth were something outside yourself that you could put on. It is simply you. To know it is to be it. That is what it means to be "one" with something.

That is how it is with God and us. Now that the veil of separation is out of the way, God takes us into His own oneness (John 17:11, 21, 22).

One with God – what can that mean?

I almost contradict myself to give an answer, because anything I say can only be a signpost or a pointer. Anyone who goes past this point must go up the mountain alone and hear God Himself.

First, one means solitary. There is only one God. To be one with the One means to be solitary in ourselves. That is, in ourselves we are not two, but one. We are two, Creator and created, but in this ardent union of two we are inseparably one. This is true of us as individuals, each individual being Christ as each, and at the same time true for the whole church in the whole world. Each member of His Body, the Church, is a different, distinct and unique member of the household of God, and yet all of us together are no other than the same One Person manifesting Himself fully in all and through all as One Christ.

There is no other except this One, who is the All in all.

One means we are in the world but not of it. We are the same Christ in us in our world regardless of the current state of our world. We live out of the Speaking (Word) of God, not the speaking (word) of our world. Everything is spoken into existence by Him, consists by Him, is upheld by Him, and yet He is to the world as the Unseen Hand, giving life and existence to everything in the world, not recognized by the world, but He is to those who love Him. We live unconsciously in One so mighty He could dissolve all things in a moment and it would be as if they never were, and yet He is so gentle and steadfast in love that He does not quench the smallest ember of faith in a piece of smoking flax, or break off a bruised stem when He passes by, for it might yet recover and grow. His sun and rain shine and fall on all, blessing everyone by and through His being. His glory shines through the good and evil in the world, for He is Himself One even in the good and evil in the world. But the world does not see Him. It does not know Him and it cannot, even though He is present in every place and state and causing all things in it to be.

However, the fact that the world does not know Him has not stopped the Father from loving the world enough to send the Lamb into it to die for it. In fact, it is because the world does not know Him that He sent His Lamb into it, and He is continuing to do so in you and me. The Father loves the world, and in Him we also love the world. We do not love its sorrow and its evil, but because we do not love those things we are free to love the world with the love of God. And where can we find love so omnipotent and filling that the universe cannot contain Him, but Who also knows when a sparrow falls and how many hairs are on each of our heads? What kind of God is that, Who is more infinite than the distances between the stars, not only in His being but in His intricate involvement in upholding all things, eternally speaking all things into existence, but knows when a sparrow falls? That is the God in which we are One.

One means that God is the same sufficiency and love in everything that is. We learn, as did Paul, to be content with lack and content with abundance, because in Him they are the same. When we know that, we know that we, too, are the same in either lack or abundance, because we find our sufficiency not in things we can see and touch, but in the imperceptible and immaterial. Nothing that comes to us is coming from only the world or from only other people, though everyday it looks like that. Everything we receive, we receive directly from God because He is the Fountainhead of all creation, and therefore the headwaters of everything. There is no other. Because all things come from God, whatever they are, they are good and perfect and we are thankful.

One means that everywhere that is, in everything that is, there is always a slain Lamb at the very center. The Word of God is an innocent and spotless Lamb, slain eternally, and it is by this Word, and therefore by this Lamb slain, that all things consist. The Lamb upholds the universe. What that means is that when we live in the oneness of God, in everything that is, the same Lamb slain is in the center, the center of everything. When one lives in the Cross, it radiates out from every center and fills up every circumference. We see everything in life participating in life and death and joy and sorrow, but through the Cross, we see death persistently vanquished and life continually raised up.

Oneness with Him means we know His perfection and completion in us manifesting in our own daily lives. When we walk and talk it is He walking and talking. To know Him is to be Him in the world.

This is what it is to "know" God. It is not learning concepts and attributes and trying to emulate them. It is not being religious, scriptural or pious. Knowing God means simply to be Him in the world. We are His containers, His vessels, and we are even more than that. We each are a temple of His in the world, a repository of the Divine Presence, yet to be One means being more than a temple that contains Him. It is more than being a branch on the True Vine. It is more than being His servant. All those things are certainly true in their place as we are helped along in our understanding toward the total.

But to know God is to be one in His oneness. The total is "one." He and I are one. One person? Yes. One heart? Yes. One mind? Yes. One Spirit? Yes. One intent? Yes. One will? Yes. One everything? YES! Jesus has brought us, through His intercession, into the same oneness He describes with the Father and the Spirit. (John 17:21-23). This is not something to "understand" intellectually. It cannot make sense that way. It is a "BE" thing. As He is, so are we in this world.

This is outside of experience as we have always known experience. We are not talking about visions and voices, or feelings of religious fervor. We may not have any of that. Walking around and living in the world IS the experience. We walk around being ourselves, unconscious of ourselves as ourselves, and that is what it is to know God. He is found in and through everything we see, hear, know, experience, and on and on beyond any description of words. With that same lack of words to describe, we say we are, through Christ, one person, one Head, Christ, expressing Himself in His many members in all we say and do by the Spirit. We know Him by living Him. We simply stand up and start walking, in worship saying, "Lord, this is you walking." We merely open our mouths and speak, in worship saying, "Lord, it is you who speaks." (John 7:17)

That is the law of the Spirit of life in Christ Jesus that now upholds us and works in us. (Is 42:1). It works of itself, as we have found to our relieved delight, and has caused us to lie down and rest in Him in green pastures. It is the kingdom of heaven grown up, we know not how. It has grown up in the most surprising of places, appearing in us even as just our plain old selves we have in some way always been, and yet we are not the same, which is truly a wonder of wonders. It is finding the "pearl of great price," or a "treasure hid in a field." (Matt 13:44-46). At first, we are as surprised as Jacob who said, "Surely God is in this place, and I knew it not." (Gen 28:16).

Surely God is in this place.

About the Author

Fred Pruitt has written about Christian spirituality for more than twenty-five years. He currently lives in Nashville, TN, with his wife Janis, a musician. Fred spends his time writing and traveling where invited, speaking and sharing about the life of Christ in us. Many of his other articles and writings are found on the worldwide web at www.thesingleeye.com, and www.christasus.com.

CPSIA information can be obtained at www.ICGtesting.com
Printed in the USA
BVOW07s2013171114

375515BV00001B/8/P